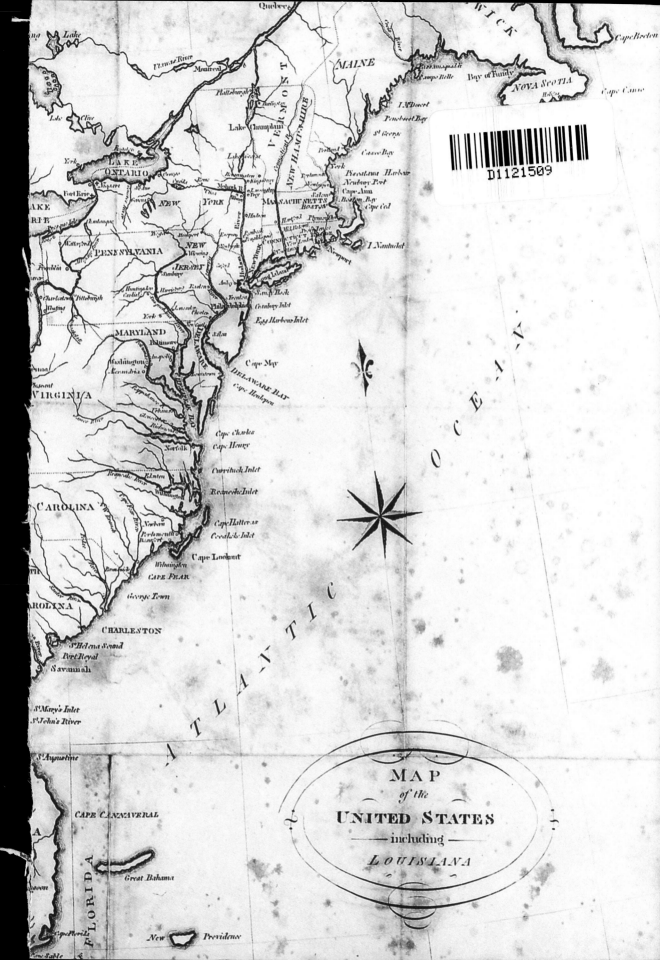

MAP
of the
UNITED STATES
— including —
LOUISIANA

The Way they Travel in the West.....See page 28.

BOOKS ON THE FRONTIER

PRINT CULTURE IN THE AMERICAN WEST

1763–1875

BY RICHARD W. CLEMENT

PUBLISHED BY

THE LIBRARY OF CONGRESS · WASHINGTON, D.C.

DISTRIBUTED BY

UNIVERSITY PRESS OF NEW ENGLAND · HANOVER AND LONDON

2003

Library of Congress Cataloging-in-Publication Data

Clement, Richard W., 1951–

Books on the frontier: print culture in the American West, 1763–1875 / by Richard W. Clement.

p.   cm.

Includes bibliographical references and index.

ISBN 0-8444-1080-2 (acid-free paper)

1. Book industries and trade—United States—History. 2. Book industries and trade—West (U.S.)—History. 3. Printing—United States—History. 4. Printing—West (U.S.)—History. 5. Books and reading—United States—History. 6. Books and reading—West (U.S.)—History. 7. Newspaper publishing—United States—History. 8. Frontier and pioneer life—United States—History. 9. United States—Territorial expansion—History. 10. West (U.S.)—History. I. Title.

Z473.C59 2003

381.45002'0973—dc21   2003003537

Designed by Robert L. Wiser, Silver Spring, Md.

Indexed by Victoria Agee

Published by the Library of Congress, Washington, D.C., 20540-4980

Distributed by University Press of New England, Hanover, New Hampshire 03755

Printed in Singapore

9   8   7   6   5   4   3   2   1

"Map of the United States, Including Louisiana." From Christian Schultz, *Travels on an Inland Voyage* (New York: Isaac Riley, 1810), foldout plate, vol. 1, p. 1. Rare Book and Special Collections Division, Library of Congress.

"The Way They Travel in the West," back cover, *Crockett Almanac* 1840, Nashville, Tenn. (i.e., Boston). Rare Book and Special Collections Division, Library of Congress.

Daniel Boone fighting a bear, from Timothy Flint, *The First White Man of the West* (Cincinnati, Ohio: Applegate and Co., 1856), 70. General Collections, Library of Congress.

D. McGowan and George H. Hildt, *Map of the United States West of the Mississippi, Showing the Routes to Pike's Peak, Overland Mail Route to California, and Pacific Rail Road Surveys* (St. Louis: Leopold Gast & Bro., 1859). Geography and Map Division, Library of Congress.

For Elizabeth, Kristina, and Susanne

Title page, drawn by Thomas Nast, engraved by Davis & Speer. From Albert Deane Richardson, *Beyond the Mississippi* (Hartford, Conn.: American Publishing Co., 1867). General Collections, Library of Congress.

CONTENTS

Sequoyah (1755–1843), the inventor of the Cherokee alphabet, was unable to read or write English or any other European language. Though his symbols derived in part from the Roman alphabet, each letter in fact represents a syllable. For instance, *A* stands for the syllable "go," and *K* stands for "tso." In 1821 he presented his "talking leaves" to the Cherokee Nation and within a few years fully two-thirds of the nation was literate.

"Se-quo-yah," from Thomas L. McKenney, *History of the Indian Tribes of North America* (Philadelphia: E. C. Biddle, 1836–44). Rare Book and Special Collections Division, Library of Congress (LC-USZ62-1292).

FOREWORD

FOR SEVERAL REASONS, it is especially fitting that the Library of Congress, the largest library and research institution in the world, sponsor the publication of Richard W. Clement's new volume, *Books on the Frontier: Print Culture in the American West, 1763–1875*. This book complements his earlier volume, *The Book in America*, which was published in 1996 as part of the Library of Congress Classics series.

Of all its holdings, the Library of Congress's collections of books, prints, photographs, and maps about American history and culture are especially strong. Drawing skillfully on the resources of the Rare Book and Special Collections Division, the Prints and Photographs Division, and the Library's general collections, Professor Clement tells a dramatic story: how books, reading, and newspapers helped shape the American frontier and how the image and idea of the frontier became an integral part of the American character and national identity.

As he points out, "books were part of the American scene from the beginning." Moreover, as his volume makes clear, books were present in many roles—as transmitters of tradition, but also as conveyors of new ideas, as sources of entertainment and inspiration, as physical objects that had to be transported across country, and as icons representing culture and learning as settlers headed westward.

As the publishing industry and book trade expanded and struggled to meet the new demand for books and reading material, Cincinnati, Ohio, became the first western center of the trade. Professor Clement provides a vivid snapshot of the young city's printers, booksellers, and publishers. Out of this milieu emerged a bookman who directed the development of the Library of Congress at an important time in its history. Ainsworth Rand Spofford, who served as Librarian of Congress from 1864 to 1897, worked in Cincinnati as a bookseller, publisher, and newspaperman from

1845 to 1861, before moving to Washington, D.C., to accept the job of Assistant Librarian of Congress.

The Center for the Book in the Library of Congress was established in 1977 to stimulate public interest in books and reading. Encouraging the study of the history of books and print culture is one of its principal aims. At a planning meeting in 1978, historian Elizabeth Eisenstein—who later served as the center's first visiting scholar—called on the center to sponsor projects that examined how the proliferation of printed materials had altered the traditional roles of the book and the written word in society. The activities to be examined, she noted, extended from authorship to reading and encompassed printing, publishing, and the distribution of printed materials.

The Center for the Book, drawing on the rich and varied collections of the Library of Congress, has contributed to the burgeoning field of the history of the book by hosting events, organizing lectures and conferences, and sponsoring publications. Alice D. Schreyer's *History of Books: A Guide to Selected Resources in the Library of Congress* (1987) is a pioneering introduction to one institution's resources for the study of book history and allied fields. More recently, the Center for the Book has sponsored the publication of *A Handbook for the Study of Book History in the United States* (2000); *Books, Libraries, Reading, and Publishing in the Cold War* (2001); and, in collaboration with the University of Massachusetts Press and the American Antiquarian Society, *Perspectives on American Book History: Artifacts and Commentary* (2002).

Working in cooperation with subject specialists throughout the Library of Congress, the center has sponsored the publication of many conference proceedings concerning the history of books and reading, such as *Literacy in Historical Perspective* (1983); *Getting the Books Out: Papers of the Chicago Conference on the Book in 19th-Century America* (1987); and *Publishing and Readership in Revolutionary France and America (1993)*.

The Center for the Book is a catalyst in the world of books and print culture. It operates primarily through partnerships with affiliated state centers, national educational and civic groups, and academic and research organizations. Information about the Center for the Book and its programs, publications, and partnership networks can be found on the Library's Web site at < www.loc.gov/cfbook>.

John Y. Cole, Director, The Center for the Book

ACKNOWLEDGMENTS

THIS WORK, like any work of scholarship, is necessarily based on the published research of those who have come before me. I am particularly indebted to Madeline B. Stern, in her pioneering book *Imprints on History: Book Publishers and American Frontiers* (1956), for her exceptional work on James D. Bemis, Jacob W. Cruger, and Anton Roman. Her work remains the standard for these frontier figures to which any serious scholar must turn. I also wish to acknowledge Leona Rostenberg, without whose support *Imprints on History* would never have been written, and who, together with Madeline Stern, has provided inspirational support for me in my own daily work in rare books librarianship.

The sections on Mathew Carey and Joseph Charless are greatly indebted to the fine historical scholarship of David Kaser of Indiana University in his books *Messrs. Carey & Lea of Philadelphia: A Study in the History of the Booktrade* (1957) and *Joseph Charless: Printer in the Western Country* (1963). The section on Cincinnati would have been impossible without Walter Sutton's groundbreaking *The Western Book Trade: Cincinnati as a Nineteenth-Century Publishing and Book-Trade Center* (1961).

My students at the University of Kansas have always provided inspiration and fresh perspectives. In particular, Tom Kreissler, a student in my 1997 History of the Book class, produced an exceptional term paper, "Books on the Overland Trail," that provided a number of examples for this publication. I am indebted to my colleagues at the Kenneth Spencer Research Library, particularly Rebecca Schulte, Sheryl Williams, and William J. Crowe, for their unstinting support and understanding during the eight years of this project.

I am grateful to the University of Kansas Hall Center for the Humanities and the University of Kansas Libraries for grants and other support to do research at the McCracken Research Library of the Buffalo Bill Historical Center in Cody, Wyoming. I wish to thank McCracken librarian Frances Clymer for her graciousness and helpfulness during my visit.

Though it is impossible to thank the many people who helped me at the Library of Congress on my several research trips, I want to acknowledge the staff of the Rare Book and Special Collections Division and its chief, Mark Dimunation, and in particular to thank Clark Evans, of the Library's Rare Book Reading Room, who was extremely helpful.

John Y. Cole, director of the Center for the Book in the Library of Congress, who has graciously written the foreword to this work, read the manuscript early on, and it has benefitted from his critique. Michael B. Winship, professor of English, University of Texas at Austin, also very kindly agreed to read the manuscript and also offered a number of excellent criticisms. I thank both of these fine scholars, but of course responsibility for the work remains my own and any errors are mine. An early version of chapter 5, "The Frontier in Books," appeared in *Publishing Research Quarterly* 14, no. 3 (1998): 53–65.

Books on the Frontier has had a difficult journey to publication. Originally conceived as a volume in the Library of Congress Classics series, the manuscript was delivered in 1997, and together with Margaret E. Wagner of the Publishing Office of the Library of Congress, I began the process of manuscript editing and selecting potential illustrations from the collections of the Library of Congress for a glitzy, illustrated trade book. In the middle of this work, the series ceased publication, and both the Library of Congress and I were left without a publisher. However, the director of the Library of Congress Publishing Office, W. Ralph Eubanks, believed in this book and worked diligently to convince University Press of New England that *Books on the Frontier* was a worthwhile project. With UPNE on board in 2002, Evelyn E. Sinclair of the Publishing Office took hold of the project and under her masterful editorial hand the book has come to publication.

No sooner had William N. Byers set out from Omaha in 1859, bound for the goldfields near Pike's Peak with a printing press and other necessary equipment, when he learned that he was not the only printer who intended to open a newspaper office in the settlement that would soon be known as Denver. Jack Merrick was two weeks ahead of him, and so Byers decided to leave his slow wagon to his journeyman printers and ride quickly ahead. Arriving in Cherry Creek, as Denver was then called, he made preparations to set up his press as soon as his wagon arrived, but he told no one of his intentions. Merrick, already in town with his own press, had yet to set it up. When the wagon rolled in and Byers almost immediately began typesetting the first issue of the *Rocky Mountain News*, Merrick, stunned at this sudden appearance of a rival press, likewise began frenetic activity to print the first issue of his *Cherry Creek Pioneer*. The race was great public entertainment until, on April 23, 1859, Byers distributed his paper twenty minutes ahead of Merrick. The *Rocky Mountain News* was also far better printed and edited than its competitor. Thoroughly defeated, Merrick sold his press, bought a pick and shovel, and headed up into the goldfields.

"An Armed Neutrality," drawn by A. R. Waud, engraved by G. H. Hayes. From Albert Deane Richardson, *Beyond the Mississippi* (Hartford, Conn.: American Publishing Co., 1867), 291. General Collections, Library of Congress.

The phrase "Westward the Course of Empire Takes Its Way" came to typify the westward movement. An eminent Irish philosopher and mathematician, Bishop George Berkeley, writing in the 1720s, penned this phrase in his poem "Destiny of America." It was repeated in various forms in America throughout the nineteenth century. Timothy Flint used a variation, "Westward the Star of Empire holds its way," on the title page of his *Indian Wars* (1833), and George Bancroft used another variant, "Westward the Star of Empire takes its way," as the epigraph to his monumental *History of the United States* (1834–75). Henry David Thoreau quoted the Bancroft version in his *Excursions* in 1862. The phrase was often attached to images, such as Emanuel Leutze's 1861 painting in the U.S. Capitol, *Westward the Course of Empire Takes Its Way*, or Andrew Melrose's 1867 painting *Westward the Star of Empire Takes Its Way: Near Council Bluffs, Iowa*, or, illustrated here, the 1868 lithograph published by Currier & Ives, *Across the Continent: Westward the Course of Empire Takes Its Way*.

Currier & Ives, *Across the Continent: Westward the Course of Empire Takes Its Way*, drawn by F. (Fanny) Palmer, lithograph, 1868. Prints and Photographs Division, Library of Congress (LC-USZ62-1).

INTRODUCTION

*We go eastward to realize history and study the works of art and
literature. . . . We go westward as into the future, with a spirit of enterprise
and adventure. . . . Eastward I go only by force; but westward I go free.*

—Henry David Thoreau, "Walking," *Atlantic Monthly* (June 1862)

FROM THE VERY FIRST, the frontier has been an integral part of the
American experience. When the early settlers stepped ashore in
Jamestown in 1607 and Plymouth in 1620, they were extending the
frontier, that elusive line of demarcation between Western civilization and
the unknown lands beyond. Unlike the frontier in Europe, the American
frontier was more than a simple boundary between states. The New World
frontier constituted a vast unknown region where the new settlers confronted an environment different from any they had lived in before. And
compounding this strangeness was the fact that this new land was populated by people quite unlike themselves. The twin challenge of finding a
way to master both the land and its inhabitants distinguished life on the
American frontier and shaped the development of a national identity that
has defined America to this day.

But even as the colonists adapted to the new environment and became
uniquely American, they also looked back to Europe and acknowledged
their deep cultural roots in the ancient traditions of Western culture.
These traditions manifested themselves in many institutions such as
churches, schools, and governing bodies, but, most importantly—and
especially for those far away from cities and institutions—European traditions were conveyed by books. And books were a part of the American
scene from the beginning.

The first colonists, many of whom were university graduates, brought large numbers of books to the New World, and by 1638 a printing press had been set up in Massachusetts. A century later there were printers working in almost every major city along the coast and in many smaller communities to the west. Though most books were still imported from London, American printers produced books and periodicals for the local market, notably newspapers and almanacs. American booksellers traded in both books imported from Europe and the products of local American printers, bringing to many remote towns both the vast and enduring wealth of Western culture and the intimate, but ephemeral, news of local events.

As the eastern seaboard settlements grew, many colonists found these new American cities too constricting and not at all unlike the cities they had left behind in Europe. When the successful conclusion of the French and Indian War in 1763 effectively opened the great hinterland—regardless of governmental proclamations to the contrary—a massive migration began flooding into Kentucky and Tennessee. At the turn of the century, the westward movement eased, but when economic troubles increased in the East in 1806, so too did the westward migration. By 1820 there were American states all along the eastern bank of the Mississippi. At the same time, something else had been created in the vast hinterland between the eastern seaboard cities and the Mississippi River, and that was a distinctly American frontier.

EUROPEAN FRONTIERS were borders between states, often fortified and often running through heavily settled regions. The American frontier, on the other hand, was a region to the west of the settled and domesticated areas in the East. At times it would encompass vast areas, but it was always shifting westward. What most clearly distinguished the American frontier was a state of mind, an outlook on life formed by its inhabitants that was markedly different from the mindset of those who remained behind. Life on the frontier was hard and full of dangers. The effort to create new homes and farms out of the wilderness, to come to terms with the native peoples of those regions, and to form communities and local governments demanded initiative and courage, self-reliance, endurance, and, finally, a belief in what came to be known as manifest destiny. On the frontier, people were valued for their actions, not for their ancestry. Alexis de Tocqueville, that extraordinarily astute Frenchman who observed American customs and institutions in the 1830s, certainly recognized the diminished importance of ancestry: "America, then, exhibits in her social state a most extraordinary phenomenon. Men are there seen on a greater equality in point of fortune and intellect, or, in other words, more equal in their strength, than in any other country of the world, or in any age of which history has preserved the remembrance."

While tens of thousands of Americans were pouring through the Cumberland Gap or rafting down the Ohio River, the American book trade was beginning a long process of consolidation and centralization based in Boston, Philadelphia, and, most of all, New York. This consolidation never completely discouraged printers from setting up in the new towns along the frontier, but the centralization of the publishing industry in the East was always a factor in a frontier printer's projects. The great publishing houses such as Harper & Brothers in New York were able to produce books and periodicals much more efficiently than any local printer in the hinterlands. On the other hand, Harper and the other houses faced the problem of getting the finished products to consumers in the back country, where roads hardly existed at all.

Most people on the frontier were literate and eager for reading material, both to learn about current events and to better themselves. In the absence of schools and other established cultural institutions, books served as the primary carriers of culture and civilization into newly settled regions, penetrating to even the most humble of homesteads. Thus there were many opportunities for the printers who carried presses and type along wilderness tracks, for the booksellers and itinerant salesmen who opened up intellectual horizons across the hinterlands, for the librarians who insisted on making books available for all, and for avid readers who eagerly read almost anything they could get their hands on.

Frontier printers and publishers produced standard works that the new communities needed, while the established publishers in the East printed the tales of frontier adventure that shaped the nation's view of the West. People on the frontier enjoyed the adventure stories of Daniel Boone, Davy Crockett, Buffalo Bill, and the others, along with the entire nation—and indeed much of the rest of the world—but locally they required the pragmatic kinds of publications that formed the underpinnings of civilized society, such as newspapers, almanacs, books of laws and statutes, schoolbooks, missionary tracts, and the like. Of course, the situation on the ground was never as distinct as such a dichotomy might suggest. We need merely consider one exceptional frontier journalist,

Mark Twain, and how his reporting of frontier life in the gold camps in the Sierra Nevada in the 1860s launched him along the path toward major literary accomplishments. In crossing over, he fashioned stories that helped shape the nation's self image.

After the 1890 census was compiled, the superintendent of the census declared that the American frontier was closed, and by the U.S. Census Bureau's narrow definition of the frontier as that area with no more than two persons per square mile, this was true. Based on the Census Bureau statement, the historian Frederick Jackson Turner proclaimed the end of the frontier. Turner quite rightly perceived the importance of the frontier in shaping America, and he believed its influence to be at an end. What he failed to see was that the image and idea of the frontier would continue to live on and would become an integral part of the nation's idea of itself, indeed creating a national vision. Through the images and stories of the American West produced by the eastern publishers in such popular series as the Buffalo Bill dime novels, or the more literary works of Owen Wister, or the illustrations of Frederic Remington and Charles Russell, the frontier qualities of self-reliance, practicality, and fortitude were seen as having created a nation distinct from all others. It was a nation based on democracy, egalitarianism, individualism, and opportunity, a nation Thomas Jefferson characterized as an empire of liberty. And however the facts of history may have punctured the vision created by this image of the frontier, such realities are hardly pertinent, as that vision, now centered on the "American Dream" that all citizens can still grasp the opportunities of the frontier and achieve prosperity, continues to motivate our nation today.

William F. Cody (1846–1917) earned his fame as a scout for the U.S. Army, winning the Congressional Medal of Honor in 1872. He earned theatrical fame as Buffalo Bill in a series of plays, such as *The Scouts of the Prairies* (1872) and *The Scouts of the Plains* (1873), in which he played himself. Lithographs such as this one were widely distributed, making the image of Buffalo Bill instantly recognizable across the nation.

The Scout Buffalo Bill, color lithograph, drawn by Paul Frenzeny; Forbes Co., lithographer, ca. 1872. Prints and Photographs Division, Library of Congress (LC-USZ62-538).

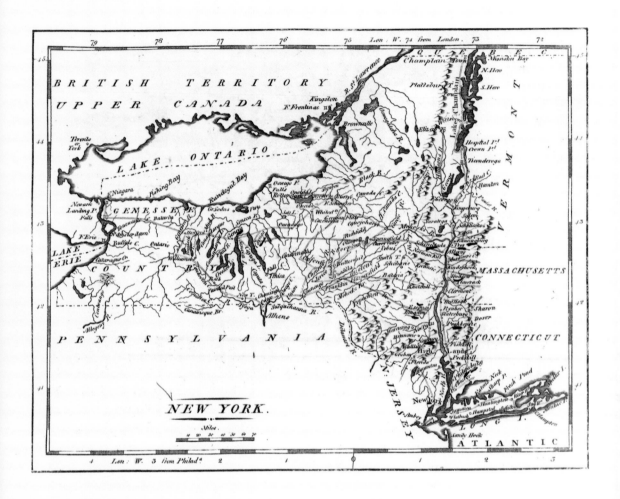

Western New York in 1803—the year James Bemis left Albany for parts west—consisted of small villages and farms surrounded by the vast frontier wilderness. Roads were almost nonexistent, as Bemis discovered while making his way toward the Canadian town of York (or Toronto). After traveling sixty-two days, he reached Canandaigua, New York, in January 1804, and in that small community at the northern end of Lake Canandaigua, he decided to settle and sell books.

Map of New York from the *American Pocket Atlas*, 3rd edition (Philadelphia: Mathew Carey, 1805). Geography and Map Division, Library of Congress.

CHAPTER ONE

THE FIRST FRONTIER

Who can tell how far it extends?
Who can tell the millions of men whom it will feed and contain?

—St. John de Crèvecoeur, *Letters from an American Farmer*, 1782

T HE AMERICAN BOOK TRADE was full of contradictions from its beginnings. It was both cohesive and disparate. Printers, publishers, booksellers, and others in the trade formed a kind of chaotic brotherhood
that functioned in a complicated network across first the colonies and
then the states and territories of the new nation. The most cohesive part
of this network was to be found in the large cities—particularly Boston,
Philadelphia, and New York—along the east coast where the sea and large
rivers afforded easy communication and transportation. The situation
inland was a far different matter. Inland roads were nearly nonexistent
and although goods, including books, found their way to virtually every
settlement in the ever-expanding West, transportation costs were so high
as to make the creation of any national book distribution network
centered on the large eastern cities impossible.

Instead, provincial centers of printing and bookselling proliferated,
including those in such towns as Hartford, Connecticut; Brattleboro,
Vermont; Burlington, New Jersey; Pittsburgh, Reading, Lancaster, and
Germantown, Pennsylvania; Cincinnati, Ohio; Dumfries, Virginia; Lexington, Kentucky; and Whitehall, North Carolina, among others. In each
of these centers, a printer would attempt to supply the needs for as large
a geographical area as costs of transportation and the physical landscape
allowed. Books in small quantities, printed in Boston or New York, or

London, would find their way to these regional centers, and conversely some books printed in these centers would find their way back to the East and to the other centers. It was common for printers and booksellers—who were often one and the same—to exchange quantities of books with each other, thus giving each a more diverse stock. In such a haphazard, uncertain way, books circulated with slow but eventual success throughout the populated regions of the new nation.

It was an imperfect, disorganized system that at times was unable to respond with sufficient speed to meet readers' needs. A case in point was the publication of Thomas Paine's *Common Sense* in Philadelphia in 1776 by Robert Bell, who found himself able to print large numbers of the book but unable to supply the demand beyond Philadelphia quickly enough. Many printers in other towns and cities, even as close as Lancaster, Pennsylvania, printed their own copies for distribution in their own areas because they were unable to get copies from Philadelphia in a timely manner. This failure of the inland transportation system was an opportunity for the frontier printer. Even as the turnpike, canal, steamboat, or railroad extended further west, there was always a place for a printer beyond the reach of efficient transportation and the growing power of the eastern publishing houses.

Almost every larger settlement on the frontier soon attracted a printer, who almost always established a newspaper. This fact was commented on with some amazement in the English *Penny Magazine* in 1841. The anonymous author, assuming an obviously jaded and superior tone, noted that as soon as a frontier community reached a certain size,

some adventurer in the printing line is attracted from a distant and older settlement, aware that the publisher of a newspaper always ranks among the leading characters of a newly-settled district. This person, who probably has never ranked higher than a journeyman typesetter, on account of the universal credit system, finds little difficulty in establishing a weekly paper ... which, to a person without capital or friends to assist him, would be out of the question in this country,—whereas in most parts of America it is the easiest thing imaginable....

In the first place it is necessary to have a building erected for a printing office, which some carpenter or other undertakes to do, and as the work is to be performed on one year's credit, thirty or forty percent, more is agreed to be given than if the money were to be forthcoming on the completion of the job. However the printer gives the carpenter promissory notes to the amount of the contract, bearing the usual rate of interest; which notes are *traded away*, as the customary phrase is, a dozen times or more before they come due,—not always at the value they bear on their face, but (according to the circumstances) at what parties may be willing to receive them at.

But a printing office is of no use unless supplied with printing-types; and the necessary amount of old worn-out types is probably procured (on credit of course), and is forthwith sent to furnish the new printing office. Hence it is that the most of these newly established papers are not only very indifferently gotten up, and abound with almost every variety of typographical error or blunder, but the types are of that character to give the whole a blurred and sorry appearance. The quality

of the paper is also of a very inferior description; nor do the subscribers, under the circumstances in which most papers are first published, either desire or expect anything but a cheap article.

One such frontier printer and bookseller was James D. Bemis, who in the winter of 1803 was traveling first by wagon and then by three-horse sleigh from Albany, New York, bound for York (Toronto), Canada, where he intended to set up a bookstore for the firm of Backus & Whiting of Albany. On January 14, 1804, he arrived in Canandaigua, a small village in the wilderness of western New York. Several "gentlemen of respectability" implored him to open his store there, even if only for the winter, and he agreed. Bemis's own account, in a letter to his sister, of his trip from Albany underscores the harsh realities of transportation on the frontier.

I again "weighed anchor," and trudged in solitude along the muddy waste, (for it is indeed solitary to have no company but swearing teamsters) 'till we reached Oneida village, an Indian settlement, where, about dark, both wagons got again mired to the hub! Zounds and alack!—what a pickle we were in! ... However, after lifting, grumbling, hollowing, and tugging three hours and a half, with the assistance of an Indian, we once more got on land. It was now ten o'clock, and no tavern within our power to reach. Cold, fatigued, and hungry, we were glad to get under shelter, and accordingly stopped at the first Indian hut we found, where there was no bed, and no victuals except a slice of rusty pork. After a night spent in yawning, dozing and

Arriving from Albany's bookselling firm of Backus and Whiting when he was twenty years old, James D. Bemis (1783–1857) spent the next half-century in the town of Canandaigua. There, he became not only a bookseller but also a newspaper and book publisher who promoted the development of western New York. Apprentices from Bemis's printing establishment moved westward themselves, taking their knowledge of the printing trade with them and making supplies of schoolbooks, almanacs, pamphlets, and various other publications available to many frontier towns.

Portrait of James D. Bemis from Charles F. Milliken, *A History of Ontario County, New York, and Its People* (New York: Lewis Historical Publishing Co., 1911), vol. 1, p. 289. General Collections, Library of Congress.

gaping, we again got under headway, . . . and we went on to Onondaga, where . . . the waggoners got discouraged, and despaired of the practicability of travelling! They accordingly stored the goods, and made the best of their way home again. Here I was obliged to remain two weeks; when a fine snow falling, I hired a man with a three horse sleigh, to carry me to Canada, and arrived at this place . . . after a "short and pleasant passage" of sixty two days from Albany!

Bemis began by setting up his book and stationery shop within the store of Henry Chapin, above Wyvill's tailor shop. He had a large assortment of books and stationery, but he also sold wrapping paper, pen-knives, corkscrews, toothbrushes, quills, playing cards, pencils, slates, scales, and mathematical instruments. Within ten months, however, he had sold his interest in the shop to Myron Holley and purchased a partnership in the only newspaper west of Utica, the weekly *Western Repository*. The paper had a circulation of about one thousand and was typically carried to its readers by postrider, as Bemis described: "The most important route was the western. . . . Imagine a small, humpback, cross-eyed, deaf old man— and you may see honest Ezra Metcalf, . . . mounted on a skunk horse, and you have the post-rider. . . . In an old-fashioned pair of saddlebags, were stowed from 150 to 200 papers. On the top of this was a small portmanteau, containing the U.S. Mail, with a padlock. . . . Thus mounted, with tin horn in hand, which he blew when he got in the saddle, he set off. . . . The arrival and departure of 'old uncle Ezra' was an event."

In 1808 Bemis's partner died, leaving him sole proprietor of the newspaper. Bemis changed the name to the *Ontario Repository*, and soon it was regarded by many as one of the nation's greatest weekly newspapers. In 1810 Bemis bought back the stock of books he had sold in his first year in Canandaigua and reentered the bookselling and stationery business with a vengeance. By the early 1820s he was supplying books, stationery, and all kinds of printing equipment and supplies to a vast region that extended as far as Detroit and Mackinac and was bringing in thirty thousand dollars a year.

His reach was explained in part by the many apprentices who had learned the trade in Bemis's house and who then had gone on to establish themselves further west. One of them, Elisha Loomis, was to go as far west as Hawaii, where he established the islands' first press. Also among these apprentices were Smith H. and Hezekiah A. Salisbury, who established the first newspaper in Erie County, the *Buffalo Gazette* in 1811; Lewis H.

Redfield, who established the *Onondaga Register* in 1814; Rosswell Haskins, a bookbinder, who managed the bookstore in A. G. Dauby's printing office in Rochester; Oran Follett, who established the *Spirit of the Times* in Batavia in 1819; Chauncey Morse, who, together with Redfield, established the *Livingston Journal* in Geneseo in 1821; and Orsamus Turner, who established the *Lockport Observatory* in 1822. Late in life Bemis reflected on his former apprentices:

Here I have lived, and from time to time spread my business over the country—to set up men in business from Onondaga to Detroit. In this way fifteen bookstores were sent abroad. I established the first presses and bookstores in Erie, Wayne, Livingston, and Onondaga counties at a pecuniary loss to myself of from 20,000 to $25,000 but with the satisfaction of knowing that I had put a goodly number of young men in active and successful business.

There remained a bond between Bemis and his former apprentices that reflected well on the master printer who in time became known as the father of the western New York press.

Bemis had married in 1807 and established himself as one of the first citizens of Canandaigua, serving for a time as president of the town. As early as 1805 he had begun to publish books, and in 1812 he added a bindery to his rapidly expanding empire. At first he specialized in religious works, the sermons and tracts of local ministers, which were eagerly purchased by their parishioners. He then branched off into missionary titles such as Richard Baxter's *Call to the Unconverted* and Isaac Watts's *Plain and Easy Catechism for Children*. Being a staunch Federalist he published political works that mirrored his own view, such as Timothy Pickering's *The Dangers of the Country!* which denounced the impending War of 1812. Bemis also catered to the needs of the local schools and published such standard school texts as Noah Webster's *American Spelling Book*, George Willson's *American Class Reader*, and Tobias Ostrander's *Elements of Numbers*.

Like most frontier printers, Bemis also produced an annual almanac, *The Farmer's Diary, or Western Almanack*, which no doubt provided him with steady

From the time of Benjamin Franklin on, the almanac, ever-popular and issued annually, was a mainstay of the frontier printer. Containing statistical and practical information on everyday life, *The Farmer's Diary, or Western Almanack* was a guaranteed source of steady income for James Bemis.

Title page from Andrew Beers, *The Farmer's Diary, or Western Almanack* (Canandaigua, N.Y.: J. D. Bemis, 1816). Rare Book and Special Collections Division, Library of Congress.

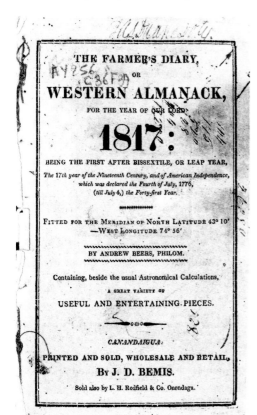

THE FARMER'S DIARY, OR WESTERN ALMANACK, FOR THE YEAR OF OUR LORD 1817:

BEING THE FIRST AFTER BISSEXTILE, OR LEAP YEAR,

The 17th year of the Nineteenth Century, and of American Independence, which was declared the Fourth of July, 1776, (till July 4,) the Forty-first Year.

FITTED FOR THE MERIDIAN OF NORTH LATITUDE 43° 10' —WEST LONGITUDE 74° 56'

BY ANDREW BEERS, PHILOM.

Containing, beside the usual Astronomical Calculations, A GREAT VARIETY OF USEFUL AND ENTERTAINING PIECES.

CANANDAIGUA: PRINTED AND SOLD, WHOLESALE AND RETAIL, BY J. D. BEMIS. Sold also by L. H. Redfield & Co. Onondaga.

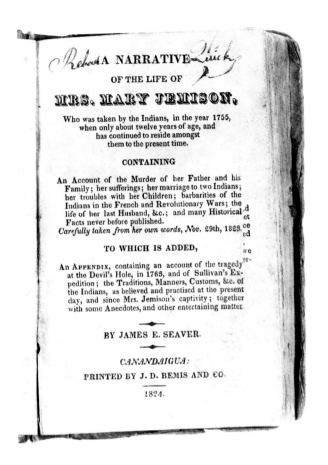

In November 1823, James Bemis and James Seaver traveled to Bethany, in Genesee County, where they interviewed Mary Jemison (1743–1833). As a girl, she had been abducted by Indians after the rest of her family was killed and had spent her whole life among the Genesee Indians, married two different men, and raised a number of children. In spite of her traumatic abduction, her life among the Genesee had been fulfilling, and she related her story to Bemis and Seaver. Seaver wrote it all down, and a few months later Bemis published *A Narrative of the Life of Mrs. Mary Jemison*. Instantly popular, the narrative proved to be Bemis's most successful book, reprinted many, many times.

James E. Seaver, *A Narrative of the Life of Mrs. Mary Jemison* (Canandaigua, N.Y.: J. D. Bemis and Co., 1824). Rare Book and Special Collections Division, Library of Congress.

and substantial income. One of the earliest items printed by the first press in the new English colonies in 1639 was an almanac, setting a pattern that remained valid for many years and in many places. In many ways the almanac was the secular equivalent of the Bible or the Book of Common Prayer. It was a guide and font of information for the coming year, and almost everyone wanted one. For a printer it was a gold mine, because it required replacement each year.

Undoubtedly the most celebrated book published by Bemis is what is known as a captivity narrative, the *Narrative of the Life of Mrs. Mary Jemison*, which was one of the few Bemis imprints that was of more than local interest. In November 1823, James E. Seaver took down the story of Mrs. Jemison, or *De-he-wa-nus*, the White Woman of the Genesee, who had been captured as a child in 1755, had seen her family murdered, and then had lived for many years among the Indians. This account, priced at thirty-seven and a half cents, was published in 1824. In that year it outsold such immensely popular works as the novels of Sir Walter Scott or James Fenimore Cooper, and throughout the rest of the decade it sold as well as the novels of those authors.

By 1825 the frontier had passed beyond Bemis and Canandaigua. The Erie Canal had arrived and with it, cheap transportation, bringing the eastern publishers, such as Harper & Brothers, who could now produce books very cheaply on a large scale in New York and ship them inland by canal boat. Regional booksellers found it easier to get new and varied stock, but frontier publishers could hardly compete. Of course, newspaper publishers continued unabated, as they provided for the local needs of the region, and such publishers might print local books now and again, but as good transportation pushed westward, it pushed the frontier and the printers westward too.

The frontier was not a single line that moved at a steady pace, all to the east being settled and all to the west being wilderness. Progressing in spurts and starts, the westward movement was like the current of a stream flowing along the most accessible paths, often leaving great islands of wilderness in its wake. Conversely there were small islands of settled regions far out to the west of the frontier, such as St. Louis or Detroit at the beginning of the century, separated from the settled states in the East by vast tracts of wilderness.

One of the major routes westward was along the Ohio River. Beginning with the Ordinance of 1787, which officially opened up the territories to the north and west of the Ohio River, large numbers of settlers began to cross the Allegheny Mountains of western Pennsylvania and move down the tributary streams of the Ohio and then along the great river itself. Most were farmers and artisans, people of limited means, who were drawn by the lure of cheap and abundant land and lucrative opportunities in the new communities. At the river, flatboats were constructed of oak planks, loaded up with whole families, livestock, and every kind of worldly possession, and then floated out on the river and pointed westward. It could be a perilous journey, and some ran afoul of the river and perished, but most came through with little loss and soon peopled the settlements that sprang up all along the river.

One such settlement was established in 1788, in a valley formed by the conjunction of the Great and Little Miami Rivers and the Ohio, 450 miles downstream from Pittsburgh. This bustling frontier trading center was Cincinnati. It attracted many settlers, among them artisans and craftsmen, and by 1793 a printer had set up shop there. William Maxwell, born in New Jersey in about 1755, traveled down the Ohio in 1790 or 1791 and settled in Lexington, Kentucky. Here he encountered John Bradford, who had set up the first press in Kentucky in 1787.

A surveyor by trade, John Bradford, had emigrated from Virginia in 1785, settling near Lexington. He readily admitted that he "had not the least knowledge of the printing business," though nonetheless in 1786 he agreed to set up a press in Lexington and establish a newspaper in exchange for a guarantee that he be given all the public printing for the territory. John Bradford and his younger brother, Fielding Bradford, went to Philadelphia, where they purchased a press, and where Fielding remained for about three months to learn as much as he could of the printing trade. Before returning to Lexington with the press, John Brad-

The challenge of navigating America's rivers—which, in the early 1800s, provided the best route for transporting a printing press or supplies of paper, as well as people—was always much greater when moving against the current. Almost any kind of boat or raft could be piloted downstream, as countless immigrants could attest, but no raft and few boats could make their way upstream against the swift currents of most American rivers. In answer to this problem, keelboats were developed in the late eighteenth century. These sturdy, narrow boats, with their shallow drafts, used oars for a downstream leg and setting poles to go upstream. Here, two varieties of keelboat ply the Mohawk River in New York.

"A View of the Boats and Manner of Navigating on the Mohawk River," from Christian Schultz, *Travels on an Inland Voyage* (New York: Isaac Riley, 1810), vol. 1, following p. 6. Rare Book and Special Collections Division, Library of Congress.

One of the most useful books printed in the West, first in Pittsburgh and then in Cincinnati, was *The Western Pilot* (earlier called *The Western Navigator*) by Samuel Cumings. Issued every several years, it provided detailed charts and instructions for navigating the constantly changing Ohio and Mississippi Rivers.

Title page from Samuel Cumings, *The Western Pilot, Containing Charts of the Ohio River, and of the Mississippi ...* (Cincinnati: Morgan, Lodge and Fisher, Printers, 1825). Rare Book and Special Collections Division, Library of Congress.

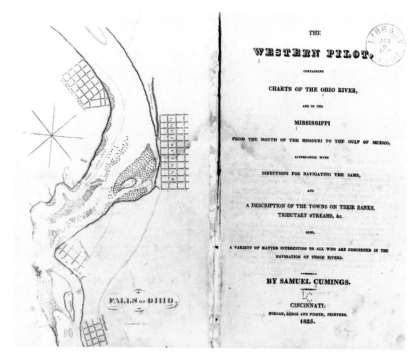

ford acquired a supply of type in Pittsburgh from John Scull, who, together with his partner Joseph Hall, had established that city's first press only a year earlier. The press and supplies were loaded on a flatboat, taken down the river, and established in Lexington. On August 11, 1787, the first issue of the *Kentucke Gazette* was issued. This was in itself quite an achievement for John Bradford, as his brother—who knew something of printing—was incapacitated, and the elder Bradford was forced by necessity to set type and print the first issue himself. But even so, the paper flourished, particularly as it was the sole newspaper west of Pittsburgh. Bradford went on to establish himself as a successful publisher and a leading citizen of Lexington, and when William Maxwell appeared in 1793, there was little opportunity for a rival printer there.

Maxwell wisely moved on to the new community of Cincinnati, where, on November 9, 1793, he published the first issue of his newspaper, the *Centinel of the North-Western Territory*. At this time Cincinnati consisted of a few framed houses and a number of log cabins along the river bank, but soon it began to acquire the marks of a literate society. Books were being advertised for sale as early as 1794 and a library was established in 1802. The first book with a Cincinnati imprint was published in 1796, *Laws of the Territory of the United States North-West of the Ohio*, which the legislature had commissioned Maxwell to print in an edition of 200 copies. Typical of the enterprising frontier printer, Maxwell decided to print five times that many and to canvass for subscribers in the *Centinel*.

He offered subscribers the discounted price of nineteen cents per fifty pages before publication as compared to thirty cents to be paid by nonsubscribers after publication. This was something of a risk for Maxwell, as his investment in paper, which had to come all the way down the river from Pennsylvania, must have been considerable. In any book the major cost was paper, which accounted for about two-thirds of a printer's investment. Maxwell succeeded getting subscribers to pay in advance and so provide him with the cash he needed to publish the book. The finished book came to 225 pages and was expertly bound by Maxwell's wife, Nancy Robins Maxwell. At about the same time, however, the printer found a far more lucrative position, becoming Cincinnati's second postmaster. He subsequently sold his newspaper and printing facilities, and in 1799 he left the book trade for a successful life in state politics.

Cincinnati was well positioned, not only as a regional center for the book trade, but for trade of all kinds. In 1793, only a few years after the community was founded, a regular keelboat packet service was established between Pittsburgh and Cincinnati. The keelboat was the only type of large boat able to go upstream; flatboats and rafts carried families and cargo downstream and were then broken up for lumber. By 1794 four boats were moving up and down the river on schedule. Working the keel-

Arriving in Cincinnati in 1793, William Maxwell (1755?–1809) founded the city's first press and established its first newspaper, the *Centinel of the North-Western Territory*. Three years later, he published the territory's first book, *Laws of the Territory of the United States North-West of the Ohio*. Maxwell received a commission from the territorial legislature to print 200 copies of the territorial laws, but he decided to print five times that number. Through his newspaper, he offered a discounted price for those who would subscribe prior to publication.

Laws of the Territory of the United States North-West of the Ohio (Cincinnati: William Maxwell, 1796), 42–43. Law Library, Library of Congress.

A Keel Boat on the Mississippi.

Keelboats grew in size and complexity, as seen in this 1838 woodcut depicting the keelboat in its prime in the early years of the century. By the early 1820s, however, the keelboat had been overtaken by the steamboat, which clearly demonstrated its seemingly effortless superiority in navigating the inland rivers.

"A Keel Boat on the Mississippi," from *Crockett Almanac* (Nashville, Tenn. [i.e., Boston], 1838), 37. Rare Book and Special Collections Division, Library of Congress.

boats was notoriously difficult and it was said that the keelboatmen were half horse and half alligator, the most famous being Mike Fink. The keelboatmen were a reckless lot who turned the waterfront of Cincinnati, and every other river city, into rough and dissolute areas that catered to almost every known vice. Yet it was the result of the labors of the keelboatmen that brought prosperity to Cincinnati, and within ten years of the founding of the town, the boats were carrying almost a million dollars worth of goods down the Ohio and the Mississippi to New Orleans, the natural outlet for the raw materials and goods produced in Cincinnati and the Northwest Territory.

In 1803 the Miami Exporting Company was founded to promote the Cincinnati-New Orleans trade. The company developed a new kind of barge that could carry a much larger load than could the narrow keelboat. It was propelled by a combination of sails, oars, and setting poles, and could carry cargo weighing from fifty to one hundred tons downstream to New Orleans and take a new, equally heavy, load back up to Cincinnati. By 1807 almost two thousand boats of all kinds arrived in New Orleans from upriver carrying cargoes worth over five million dollars.

During this period Cincinnati grew at a steady rate and began to acquire the attributes of a cultured community. Schools, of course, had been established early on, and by 1806 specialty classes in singing and dancing were being offered. Lancaster Seminary was founded in 1814 and

Crockett Almanac '38

Mike Fink, the Ohio Boatman.

Keelboatmen were notorious in every river town, and none was more famous than Mike Fink, whose exploits were known up and down the river. Notices announcing Fink's death in 1823 quickly appeared in newspapers, but it was not until the Pittsburgh newspaperman Morgan Neville wrote the first extended treatment of his life, "The Last of the Boatmen," published in Cincinnati in *The Western Souvenir: A Christmas and New Year's Gift for 1829,* that his adventures found their way into print. The following year, 1830, Timothy Flint wrote a long piece in his *Western Monthly Review*. Mike Fink's greatest popularity, however, coincided with enthusiasm for Davy Crockett in the 1840s and 1850s, when more than twenty new tales of Fink's exploits appeared, often published in the popular *Crockett Almanacs*.

"Mike Fink, the Ohio Boatman," from *Crockett Almanac* (Nashville, Tenn. [i.e., Boston], 1838), back cover. Rare Book and Special Collections Division, Library of Congress.

five years later became Cincinnati College. The first medical school west of the Alleghenies, the Medical College of Ohio, was founded in Cincinnati in 1821, and Lane Theological Seminary opened its doors in 1829. Beginning in 1819 the Haydn Society presented a concert series and the Western Museum offered classes in drawing, which, in 1820, were taught by curator John James Audubon. Shakespeare was popular, and beginning in the 1820s various traveling companies gave the citizens of Cincinnati the opportunity to see a number of plays during regular seasons.

Books, imported from the East, had long been available through a number of merchants, such as John W. Browne and Company which operated a combination drug and book store next door to the offices of the newspaper *Liberty Hall*. The first Cincinnati bookseller who sold nothing but books and stationery was John Corson, who set up shop in 1812.

Advertisements filled the otherwise blank pages at the back of books of all sorts, providing publishers with additional income. The Cincinnati Reading Room, where, for four dollars a year, subscribers could find the latest newspapers as soon as they arrived, is featured in pages at the back of an edition of *The Western Pilot* published in 1825 in Cincinnati. Conveniently located behind the post office, the room was designed to be a popular meeting place.

Advertisement page from Samuel Cumings, *The Western Pilot, Containing Charts of the Ohio River, and of the Mississippi* ... (Cincinnati: Morgan, Lodge and Fisher, Printers, 1825), 134. Rare Book and Special Collections Division, Library of Congress.

134   ADVERTISEMENTS

C. W. GAZZAM,
COMMISSION MERCHANT;
Corner of Commercial & Loring's Row,
CINCINNATI.

IRWIN & WHITEMAN,
General Agents and Commission Merchants,
NO. 2, NOBLE'S ROW,
CINCINNATI.

CINCINNATI READING ROOM.

THE Cincinnati Reading Room is furnished with the best newspapers, and literary journals of the U. States; all of which are received by the most direct conveyances. Those who are desirous of obtaining the latest intelligence can find it here. Strangers have always found, and acknowledged it an entertaining resort—and not among the least inducements for the prolongation of their visits in this city. From this consideration, if no more, the room should receive the patronage of the public.

The subscription prices are low; they have been fixed with the view to suit the times, and to accomodate those who may wish to enjoy the privilege of the Room.

The Annual Subscription, if paid at the time of subscribing, is	$4 00
Paid after, or at the end of the year,	5 00

Those who may wish to frequent it for a shorter time, can do so by paying in advance, for six months, $2 25
Three do. 1 25
One do. 50
Per week, 25

These, if not paid in advance, will be proportionably increased. Those who do not subscribe, but are enjoying the benefits of the room, will be charged according to the time they frequent it.

No subscription will be discontinued without previous notice to that effect.

The Room is on Third street, immediately back of the Post Office.

ELAM P. LANGDON, *Proprietor.*

Corson found the Cincinnati market too unresponsive to support his endeavor, however, and he soon began to offer other merchandise until his store was indistinguishable from any of a number of general stores in the city, with the exception of one innovation. In August 1813, he opened a circulating library, an obvious option for a bookseller unable to move a sizable stock. What he was unable to sell, he could now rent. How successful this venture was remains unclear, but as he closed a few years later, it may be that Corson's library was as unsuccessful as his bookstore. Even so, there were no doubt many grateful citizens of Cincinnati who found new books to read and through those books discovered the riches of Western culture, even though they lived far out on the edge of the frontier.

By 1815 Cincinnati boasted two newspapers, each of which had the capacity to publish books. Writing in 1826, Timothy Flint, a well-known minister and one of Cincinnati's leading authors and literary men, noted that "efforts to promote polite literature have already been made in this town" and by 1815 "There were ... two gazettes, and two booksellers' shops, although unhappily novels were the most saleable article." Booksellers had a ready market, but the lack of paper presented a major impediment to the growth of book publishing.

A small paper mill had been established as close as Georgetown, Kentucky, in 1793, but its limited output was all but taken up by the printers in nearby Lexington. With supplies limited to what arrived by riverboat, even newspaper publication was on occasion suspended. In one instance, the *Liberty Hall and Cincinnati Mercury* for January 6, 1807, almost did not appear because of a lack of large-size paper: "It is with extreme regret that the editor is obliged to issue the present number on a writing-sheet, occasioned by a disappointment in the receipt of paper. He hopes it will be the only instance which will occur, as his son is now in Kentucky for the express purpose of purchasing a supply of that necessary article." Eighteen months later the same editor, John W. Browne, implored his readers to pay up their subscriptions. He realized that they failed to pay not so much because they refused, but simply because there was very little money in circulation. He asked them to "furnish the Editor with a little [money], to send to the Paper-mill; otherwise he is apprehensive that *Liberty Hall* will sink for want of a few dollars to prop it. 'Tis hard to print and get nothing, and find paper in the bargain." Under such circumstances there were very few books printed.

The situation changed considerably in 1811 when two paper mills were established on the Little Miami River. In 1815 Cincinnati booster Daniel Drake noted:

Ten years ago, there had not been printed in this place a single volume; but since the year 1811, twelve different books, besides many pamphlets, have been executed. These works, it is true, were of moderate size; but they were bound, and averaged more than 200 pages each. The paper used in these offices was formerly brought from Pennsylvania, afterwards from Kentucky, but at present from the new and valuable paper mills on the Little Miami.

Although the city's first bookbinder, George T. Williamson, had set up business in 1806, it was the opening of the local paper mills and the subsequent blossoming of book publishing that stimulated the binding trade. By 1818 several bookbinders were working in Cincinnati, sometimes operating out of the same establishment as booksellers. Many books that arrived on the quayside were still bundled in unbound sheets. Traditionally a purchaser would take his or her book, still in sheets, to a binder who would fold and sew the sheets and then bind the book in leather according to the customer's wishes. By 1820 many booksellers offered almost all of their books already bound, though a leather binding added considerably to the cost of a book.

Within ten or fifteen years all this would change. In the mid-1820s, the large eastern publishers began to introduce cloth-covered bindings (actually casings) that were attractive and durable, and most of all, very cheap. Soon virtually all books arrived from the eastern publishers already bound, and the bookbinders in frontier communities like Cincinnati found themselves restricted to binding those books published locally. Many bookbinders left the trade for better prospects in the West, or shifted to another aspect within the trade such as bookselling.

By 1818 Cincinnati, with a population of nine thousand, was the largest city in the West and was developing a more vibrant book trade. That year the booksellers Ferguson and Sanxay advertised "Books—Military, Mathematical, Musical, and Mercantile." In October, the firm, which included occasional publishing and bookbinding, prepared a prospectus for a very ambitious project, the works of the ancient historian Josephus, translated by William Wiston, to be sold by subscription. Local publishing had long been confined to works of strictly local interest, and indeed Ferguson and Sanxay had profited greatly in publishing such local items as *The Farmers Almanack*, an edition of which for 1819 had just been completed and offered for sale in the previous month. The works of an ancient Latin author such as Josephus was another thing entirely. This was the sort of title more often published in New York or London, but even so the local press was enthusiastic and noted that the venture was "of greater magnitude than has been attempted by any bookseller [i.e., publisher] this side of the Ohio: should they succeed, it is the intention of the publishers to make the work a flattering specimen of the art of printing in the west." The publishers soon found they had overreached themselves and that very few readers in Cincinnati were interested in subscribing to the works of Josephus, regardless of how finely printed. Without subscribers, the book was never published.

Despite the failure of such an ambitious project, the attempt indicates that there were those who would have been more than happy to read such a tome, and many other similar volumes as well. It was for these active readers that the bookseller George Charters opened a large circulating library in November 1818. The library of three thousand volumes consisted of history, travels, voyages, lives, reviews, magazines, novels, romances, tales, plays, and other genres of fiction and nonfiction. Charters must have succeeded where others before him had failed as he remained in business until 1825, a far longer time than most of his fellow booksellers.

Charters was not without competitors. In 1819, T. Reddish, an Englishman, who had been in the trade in Philadelphia for some years, established the Sun Circulating Library with a collection of books imported from England. He noted in the press: "T. R[eddish] flatters himself that in consequence of the above Library being just imported from England, it consequently contains a number of original works never yet published in the United States, therefore very scarce, or not at all to be met with in any other Public Library." Certainly by the 1820s books of all kinds were to be easily had in Cincinnati.

Of course, the Cincinnati book trade did not function in isolation. For example, when William Hill Woodward opened his bookstore in 1820, he emphasized his father's established bookselling and publishing business in Philadelphia: "By his connexion with his father, W. W. Woodward, he will be able to execute orders to any amount without the delays to which the residents of these parts have heretofore been subject." Woodward made the most of his connection and flourished. And, indeed, most of the books that were sold and read in Cincinnati were published in the East and brought down the Ohio River. The local booksellers had no choice but to work with the eastern firms if they were to obtain a diverse stock.

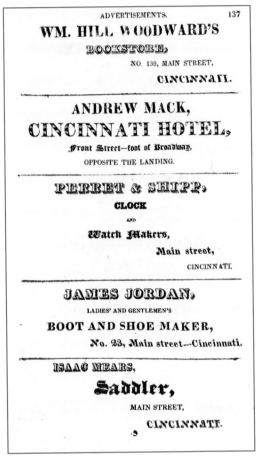

Trading with the established publishing houses in the East was bedeviled not only by the logistical problems of getting the books across mountains and down rivers, but most of all by the lack of sound currency in the West. Banks in every city and town issued notes that circulated as currency, which created a fairly chaotic and unstable system. Although western currency was usually sound enough within the western regions, it was heavily discounted in the East. Thus when a merchant from Cincinnati attempted to pay for eastern goods with Cincinnati currency, his dollars were worth something less than face value, if he could use the notes at all.

A case in point was the Cincinnati firm of Phillips and Speer, which had a long-standing relationship with the firm of the great Philadelphia publisher Mathew Carey (who operated as Carey & Son with his son Henry, and later as H. C. Carey & Lea). During the first decades of the century, Philadelphia was the first city of the American book trade (though New York would overtake it by 1830) and it was the most natural geographical point of contact for the booksellers and publishers down the Ohio River. Records of the business relationship between the two firms illustrate how difficult the trade was, primarily because of the Cincinnati firm's inability to obtain eastern notes. Carey sold stock on credit and as notes came due asked for payment. For example, in January 1816, Carey & Son asked for payment of a note for $800 which had come due in November. The problem was that "Philadelphia paper is not to be had in [Cincinnati] for any price," and the booksellers offered to make the payment in Cincinnati currency at face value. Carey suggested they pay in stamps, which was an acceptable arrangement, but not a permanent solution.

Times were good and firms like Phillips and Speer managed one way or another to buy books in the East and sell them in the West. During the winter of 1818–19, however, a financial panic developed. The Cincinnati booksellers wrote to Carey:

You have no doubt been apprised of the Banks in this town stopping specie payment and of the impossibility of our paying our notes in the U.S. Branch. We have $1,000 deposited in the M[iami] E[xporting] Company office to pay our note and the draughts collected by us which shall remain there until we hear from you. We hope some arrangements can be made to prevent loss to either of us.

On December 17, 1818, they wrote again:

Our note was presented for payment in U.S. notes or specie which it was impossible to procure. We offered to pay in Cincinnati money which was refused. We have the money in bank. Can you draw on us through men moving to this country

William Hill Woodward's bookstore on Main Street, Cincinnati, was established in 1820 and long served as a focal point for people with literary interests. Woodward was the son of W. W. Woodward, the successful Philadelphia bookseller, a connection that provided the younger Woodward with an advantage in obtaining books from the East, particularly in times of financial turmoil.

Advertisement page from Samuel Cumings, *The Western Pilot, Containing Charts of the Ohio River, and of the Mississippi* ... (Cincinnati: Morgan, Lodge and Fisher, Printers, 1825), 137. Rare Book and Special Collections Division, Library of Congress.

or any other way that will not subject us to losses that we are totally unable to bear—could our draught on the Miami E[xporting] Company be negotiated in any bank in Philadelphia for 2 or 2½ percent.

The crisis deepened and eastern money could be had only for a 20 percent premium or more, if at all. Still commerce was maintained as Carey continued to ship books to Cincinnati through the spring of 1819, and the booksellers were able to make a few small payments in eastern currency. On March 15, the booksellers wrote Carey: "We hope that the present unavoidable delay in our payments will not prevent your sending the articles ordered by us some time since; arrangements will shortly be made that cannot fail to satisfy you." Regardless of those arrangements, by late summer the firm was unable to purchase any more books and during the next six months was unable to obtain eastern currency even at a premium of 20 percent. In June 1820, the firm's Cincinnati bank failed, and Phillips and Speer were confronted with the possibility of a loss of $2,000. The bank's "paper fell to 25 cents per dollar & the only chance we had of saving ourselves was to vest it in property which we have done."

Mathew and Henry Carey were alarmed at the turn of events and instructed their new partner, Isaac Lea, to visit Cincinnati and evaluate the situation. Lea arrived in the spring of 1821 and found the booksellers had been accurate in their reports concerning the financial crisis. Lea first obtained a mortgage on the Cincinnati property in which Phillips and Speer had invested the money intended for Carey & Lea, and then the booksellers suggested that they pay off the rest of the debt "by forwarding printing paper, or which we think the most advantageous to both parties, printed books, if you can propose any works you wish printed, we can execute it for you and deliver it in Philadelphia in sheets, or folded and sewed, at the same prices you now pay." They were able to supply Carey with $2,000 worth of paper every six months from their paper mill, but they preferred to work the debt off by printing books as well, because paper was far more valuable as a readily salable item in the West.

On April 26, 1821, Carey agreed to the suggestion that Phillips and Speer supply him with paper and undertake printing for him. It is remarkable, given the distances involved, that the nation's premier publisher would contract with a firm out on the edge of the frontier to supply paper and provide printing. But under the extreme circumstances of the economic depression and the resultant lack of currency, such an arrangement was but one of many innovative schemes put forward by publishers and booksellers in their efforts to remain solvent.

Carey wanted to move books and offered the Cincinnati booksellers a line of credit of five to ten thousand dollars a year, but the partners were more interested in promoting the papermaking side of their business. "We have procured the use of a steam engine for our paper mill on advantageous terms which will allow us to manufacture a much larger quantity than we could have done on our original plan. We believe it would not be doing justice to you or ourselves to purchase books at this time." By early July 1821, the Cincinnati Steam Paper Mill was operating. At the same time the firm began work on two printing projects for Carey & Lea.

The first of these projects was a traditional law book, William Salkeld's *Reports of Cases Adjudged in the Court of King's Bench* containing cases from 1689 to 1712, a standard item in any lawyer's library. This three-volume set was to be printed in Cincinnati on locally produced paper and shipped in sheets to Philadelphia, where a title page would be added. It would then be distributed from Philadelphia and New York through the normal channels, a few finding their way back to the West (though it would have been remarkable had Phillips and Speer not arranged to reserve a few copies for sale in Cincinnati, but necessarily supplying their own title page).

The second project made better use of Cincinnati's geographical position. Carey & Lea had agreed to supply the Pittsburgh firm of Patterson and Lambdin with large quantities of Webster's *American Spelling Book*, and it made sense to have Phillips and Speer in Cincinnati fulfill this order for the Philadelphia publisher. The Cincinnati firm did not print the spellers, but acted to obtain as many as could be purchased through local contacts. The partners were able to purchase copies at $1.50 a dozen and in April 1822 sent 1,320 copies to Pittsburgh.

Meanwhile, the printing of Salkeld's *Reports* proceeded slowly. On January 22, 1822, the first substantial shipment of sheets was sent to Philadelphia, and by the end of the year the three-volume set appeared. But all was not smooth sailing in the relationship between the two firms. Perhaps because the printing of Salkeld's *Reports* was taking so much time, Carey & Lea threatened to sue the Cincinnati firm in about May 1822. The booksellers promised to make monthly payments, but were unable to pay the $300 per month required.

In October new arrangements were made in which Phillips and Speer agreed to pay Carey & Lea monthly payments and to make regular shipments of paper to the firm of Pennoyer & McKean in New Orleans that would be credited to the Philadelphia firm. In addition, they were to continue sending copies of Webster's speller to Pittsburgh. But even this arrangement fell apart as Phillips and Speer sent a new shipment of spellers upriver, not knowing that the Pittsburgh firm of Patterson and Lambdin, destined to receive them, had just failed. In June 1823, Carey complained that there was no way to recover the value of the lost books because Patterson and Lambdin had never been charged for them; Phillips and Speer would have to pay.

At this point the correspondence between the firms ends, and we are unable to look further over the shoulders of these pioneer booksellers, printers, publishers, and papermakers in Cincinnati. But as the firm was active through the 1820s and much of the 1830s, we can conclude that they survived this small crisis, and no doubt many others, as they struggled to bring books to the West.

It was not unnatural that as the largest city in the West, Cincinnati should become the publishing capital for the region. The city's publishing output was almost entirely for local and regional consumption, and, as already mentioned, local almanacs were among the most steady and reliable sources of income. Another important genre of publication was the emigrant guide, which was produced both to attract settlers and to provide them with information about the routes West. Two of the earliest produced in Cincinnati were *The Emigrant's Guide, or Pocket Geography of the Western States and Territories*, which Phillips and Speer produced in 1818, and Edmund Dana's *Geographical Sketches on the Western Country: Designed for Emigrants and Settlers*, which was published by Looker, Reynolds, and Company in 1819. In a similar category was the river guide, which provided up-to-date information on the course of the Ohio and other rivers, including detailed charts and maps. The rivers were the major highways for settlers and merchants alike, and they were unmarked for navigation. The river guides were first published in Cincinnati in 1825, under the title *The Western Pilot*, and continued publication on a nearly annual basis until the 1870s.

Authoritative guidebooks were in great demand, particularly those published in the West. Edmund Dana's *Geographical Sketches on the Western Country: Designed for Emigrants and Settlers*, published in Cincinnati in 1819, provided the new emigrant with factual and practical information on routes and available land.

Title page from Edmund Dana, *Geographical Sketches on the Western Country: Designed for Emigrants and Settlers* (Cincinnati: Looker, Reynolds, and Co., 1819). Rare Book and Special Collections Division, Library of Congress.

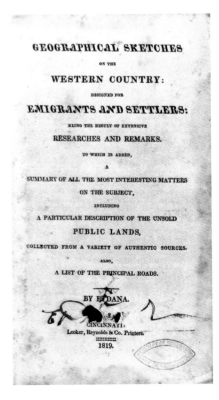

GEOGRAPHICAL SKETCHES

ON THE

WESTERN COUNTRY:

DESIGNED FOR

EMIGRANTS AND SETTLERS:

BEING THE RESULT OF EXTENSIVE

RESEARCHES AND REMARKS.

TO WHICH IS ADDED,

A

SUMMARY OF ALL THE MOST INTERESTING MATTERS

ON THE SUBJECT,

INCLUDING

A PARTICULAR DESCRIPTION OF THE UNSOLD

PUBLIC LANDS,

COLLECTED FROM A VARIETY OF AUTHENTIC SOURCES.

ALSO,

A LIST OF THE PRINCIPAL ROADS.

BY E. DANA.

CINCINNATI:

Looker, Reynolds & Co. Printers.

1819.

The Missouri Harmony was one of the first tunebooks printed in the West, where it was compiled and first published in 1820 by Allen D. Carden in St. Louis. This 1825 edition was printed by Morgan, Lodge, and Fisher in Cincinnati rather than in St. Louis because of the difficulties inherent in printing musical notation. In 1827 the tunebook was again printed in Cincinnati, by the firm of Drake and Conclin. Realizing how popular it was, its compiler and publisher revised and then stereotyped the book in 1829. From the stereotype plates, Morgan and Sanxay produced a steady stream of editions in the 1830s. Highly influential, *The Missouri Harmony* served as a model for many other tunebooks, such as the *St. Louis Harmony* (1831) and the *Southern Harmony* (1835).

Title page, *The Missouri Harmony* (Cincinnati: Morgan, Lodge, and Fisher, 1825). Music Division, Library of Congress.

THE MISSOURI HARMONY,
OR A CHOICE COLLECTION OF
PSALM TUNES, HYMNS AND ANTHEMS,
SELECTED FROM THE MOST EMINENT AUTHORS, AND WELL ADAPTED TO ALL CHRISTIAN
CHURCHES, SINGING SCHOOLS, AND PRIVATE SOCIETIES;

TOGETHER WITH

An Introduction to Grounds of Music, the Rudiments of Music, and plain Rules for Beginners.

BY ALLEN D. CARDEN.

CINCINNATI.
PUBLISHED BY MORGAN, LODGE, AND FISHER.
::::::::::::
1825.

Literary works and songbooks were also part of the city's output. *The Missouri Harmony* was printed in Cincinnati in 1820 by Morgan, Lodge and Fisher, though published in St. Louis. It was reprinted many times. Another popular songbook was *The Eolian Songster*, published by U. P. James in 1832, and also reprinted for many years. The first volume of poetry to appear in Cincinnati was *The American Bards: A Modern Poem in Three Parts*, published by Phillips and Speer in 1820. It was a slim volume of fifty-two pages, which was lauded in the press as "the finest specimen of typography we have seen west of the mountains."

Of general interest were Timothy Flint's *Condensed Geography and History of the United States, or the Mississippi Valley*, which was published in Cincinnati in 1828, and his *Indian Wars of the West*, which appeared in 1833. Author of several other such historical, geographical, and topographical works on the West, Timothy Flint also edited the *Western Monthly Review*, originally the *Western Magazine and Review* (1827–30). Even earlier, Cincinnati could boast of a literary magazine, the *Literary Gazette*, which was published from 1819 to 1820, followed by *Olio* (1821–22), and the *Cincinnati Literary Gazette* (1824–25).

The *Western Monthly Review* was quite a success in terms of the articles included, but Flint struggled with the perennial problem of periodical publishers: getting his subscribers to pay. On September 28, 1828, he noted, having just returned from "the Atlantic country, . . . that three quarters of the amount of subscription from the commencement are still due. . . . The accounts of subscribers so delinquent, after a short interval, will be put into the hands of an attorney for collection, without respect of persons, and without further notice." Such threats seem to have had little effect. In May 1829, he wrote,

great numbers of our western subscribers ... have paid nothing. ... We request such people to regain their self respect. ... The Mississippi is formed by the concurrence of rivulets. Three or four dollars are, no doubt, a trifle to the subscriber; but two thousand dollars of outstanding debts would be a matter of consequence to us. It is painful, in the extreme, to us, to be compelled to make such appeals to the honour of our subscribers; but our duty to our paper maker and printer is more imperative, than any of the restraining impulses of false delicacy.

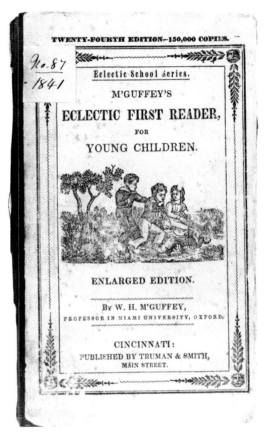

This appeal, too, seemed to fall on deaf ears, as Flint continued in April 1830:

Beloved, I so call you, because it is my vocation, and a habit. But there would be more sincerity in the phrase, if you had all paid me. ... I print my terms on every cover; and I challenge human speech to make them plainer. ... The withholding your individual subscription may be a trifle, and a sport to you; but the deficit of the sum is death to me. ... I propose, in the last number of the third volume, beloved, to make out a list of my delinquent subscribers.

The list never appeared, though Flint probably received very few back subscriptions. Instead, Flint announced that the *Western Monthly Review* was to be reorganized and changed into a quarterly. This made sense, both financially and editorially. The four issues of a quarterly were less expensive to produce than the twelve monthly issues, and the constant editorial pressure for new articles and the ever-present monthly deadlines were likewise eased. Unfortunately, the *Review's* debts had grown too large, and Flint was unable to launch his new quarterly.

Not surprisingly, Flint came to know Thomas and Frances Trollope (parents of the novelist Anthony Trollope) when they stayed in Cincinnati during the same years in which Flint edited the *Review*. The Trollopes had hoped to make a success out of a mercantile venture in the city, but having little luck were forced eventually to return to England. Out of that experience Frances Trollope wrote her first successful work, *The Domestic Manners of the Americans*, which was very well received in England but generally criticized in America for dwelling on the more vulgar aspects of American society.

Whatever the merits of the work as a whole, Trollope's portrait of Timothy Flint was highly flattering. She describes him as a man of intelligence, cultivation, and literary taste, calling him "the most agreeable acquaintance I made in Cincinnati, and indeed one of the most talented men I ever met. . . . His conversational powers are of the highest order: he is the only person I remember to have known with first-rate powers of satire, and even sarcasm, whose kindness of nature and of manner remained perfectly uninjured." This was not only high praise for Flint, but also an indication that Cincinnati was becoming a cultural center that was not too far behind the eastern cities.

The single category of book for which Cincinnati publishers were best known was the schoolbook, and by 1825, when Ohio passed its first common-school law, such books made up over half of the city's output. As we have already seen, Webster's *American Spelling Book* figured prominently among these titles. Other titles were Samuel Kirkham's *English Grammar in Familiar Lectures*, Lindley Murray's *English Grammar*, and James Hall's *Western Reader*. But the schoolbook that made Cincinnati famous was *McGuffey's Reader*.

In 1834 the Cincinnati firm of Truman & Smith launched its "Eclectic Series of School Books." In 1836 the publishers contracted with William Holmes McGuffey, a professor of languages, philology, and philosophy at nearby Miami University in Oxford, Ohio, to produce four readers. McGuffey already had the first and second readers in manuscript and agreed to produce the third and fourth within eighteen months. Truman & Smith agreed to pay McGuffey a royalty of 10 percent up until he received $1,000, at which time the readers became the sole property of the publishers. In 1841 McGuffey agreed to a similar contract in which he was to produce the *McGuffey Rhetorical Reader* in return for $500. Under normal circumstances, the author had obtained good terms, but the *McGuffey Readers* were not ordinary schoolbooks.

The small firm of Truman & Smith found it had a runaway bestseller on its hands. A huge increase in sales necessitated increases in staff, which

In 1836, the Cincinnati firm of Truman & Smith published the first *McGuffey's Reader*. It was immediately so popular that by 1838 the firm had increased to thirty employees and had printed almost three hundred thousand copies on water-powered presses. By the end of the century, more than 122 million copies of the readers had been sold in over 200 editions. Generations of American school-children grew up with the McGuffey series and many made its moral values their own, thus making McGuffey an integral part of the American experience.

Front cover, William H. McGuffey, *The Eclectic First Reader*, 24th ed. (Cincinnati: Truman & Smith, 1841). Rare Book and Special Collections Division, Library of Congress.

by 1838 had grown to more than thirty, and the introduction of water-powered presses. By this time the firm had sold almost 300,000 copies and orders were flooding in. The eastern firms, who had dominated the schoolbook market in the West, began to panic as they saw their share of the western market vanish.

Unwilling to give up such a lucrative market, the eastern firms, led by Benjamin F. Copeland and Samuel Worcester of Boston, brought suit against Truman & Smith and McGuffey in October 1838. The charge was made that McGuffey had copied sections of his readers directly out of *Worcester's Second*, *Third*, and *Fourth Readers*, and had taken over the plan for his third and fourth readers directly from Worcester's identically named volumes. The easterners, in anticipation of suppressing McGuffey, arranged with the Cincinnati firm of E. Lucas and Company to sell quantities of *Worcester's Readers* and *Emerson's Class Readers*. Another local firm, Ely & Strong, advertised that they were now printing quantities of *Emerson's Class Readers* from their own stereotype plates, thus at least printing an eastern schoolbook in the West. But McGuffey and Truman & Smith were not about to give up. McGuffey quickly revised the readers so that they no longer resembled *Worcester's Readers*, and Truman & Smith paid Worcester $2,000 to drop the lawsuit.

From this point on there was no stopping the *McGuffey Readers*, now styled as the "Standard School Books of the West." By 1839 almost 500,000 had been sold, and by 1841 more than 700,000 copies in the Eclectic Series had been sold. Truman & Smith trumpeted this fact as the "strongest possible evidence of their superiority over other schoolbooks" and assured the public that "the demand for these books is very heavy; but none need apprehend that the supply will not be commensurate with the demand." Indeed by 1900, more than 122,000,000 copies of the *McGuffey Readers* had been sold.

Even after Chicago overtook Cincinnati as the West's principal city and commercial hub, schoolbook publishing continued to be one of Cincinnati's commercial strengths. With Truman & Smith leading the way, Cincinnati became the schoolbook publishing capital of the West. But by the 1830s and 1840s the frontier had long passed by Cincinnati, and what was known as "the West" was again something different.

CHAPTER TWO

TO THE MISSISSIPPI
AND BEYOND

Westward the Star of Empire holds its way.

—Timothy Flint, *Indian Wars of the West*, 1833

SOME PRINTERS AND BOOKSELLERS who moved along with the frontier achieved a measure of fame as the first to print in a particular place or region. One of these was Joseph Charless, an Irish immigrant who had arrived in Pennsylvania in about 1794. Intrigued by the West, he soon made a sortie down "the western waters, as low down the Ohio as the rapids, where a few stores and taverns constituted Louisville a town." Upon his return eastward in the summer of 1795 he settled in Lewistown, a former Shawnee village in central Pennsylvania on the Juniata River that catered to the sizable traffic moving east and west over the Juniata Path through the Alleghenies. Here he established a newspaper and bookstore. His source of books was another Irish immigrant, Mathew Carey of Philadelphia, whom we have already encountered through his connections to the Cincinnati book trade. Carey, the nation's first modern publisher, had opened his home to his fellow countryman and introduced the young printer to the American book trade.

With his new contacts in the trade and Carey's friendship, Charless was well positioned to make a success of his own venture. Letters from Charless to Carey expressed his initial optimism. In October 1795 he wrote, "I could sell a vast quantity on credit, if I had a large store which I will endeavor to accomplish, the store keepers here will sell no more books, but leave me the exclusive sale of them." Carey advanced Charless a good many books on credit, but apparently Charless was unable to move them in the quantities he had originally hoped. Compounding his lack of book sales was the perennial problem of all frontier newspaper publishers of getting his subscribers to pay. By March 1796, not only were more than half of his subscribers in arrears, but Charless held a large quantity of books that he had been unable to sell and for which he owed Mathew Carey over one hundred pounds. Facing ruin, he soon sold the whole printing establishment and left Lewistown, perhaps for Ireland.

In 1797, however, Joseph Charless was once more back in Philadelphia publishing books. He worked both as a publisher in his own right and as a printer for other publishers, particularly Mathew Carey, up until the end of 1802, with some measure of success. But he was never contented in Philadelphia and he yearned for the greater opportunities to be found in the West. In early 1803 he arrived in Lexington, Kentucky, bringing with him a complete printing establishment, a large quantity of books and stationery, and his whole household, including his wife and children. It had not been an easy journey down the Ohio in winter, but even worse was a substantial loss, which was recorded in the *Kentucky Gazette* on January 11, 1803.

Lost on Thursday last, between Licking river and Galbreath's tavern, A PILLOW CASE, containing Two POCKET BOOKS & SUNDRY BANK NOTES On the banks of the Baltimore and Wilmington, with some articles of Clothing, &c. TEN DOLLARS will be paid on the delivery of the above articles to Mr. Charles Gallagher, Limestone, or to the subscriber in Lexington. JOSEPH CHARLESS.

There is no indication that Charless ever recovered his loss.

In 1803, Lexington was the largest town in the West, not to be overtaken by Cincinnati for some years. It had a population of about three thousand, and many of its buildings and homes were made of brick. The community was a vibrant and prosperous one that already supported two newspapers, and Charless immediately founded its third, the *Independent Gazetteer*. He established himself on Main Street between the printing office of John Bradford (Kentucky's first printer), whose son Daniel published the *Kentucky Gazette*, and Captain Henry Marshall's tavern. Here he intended to publish his newspaper and sell books.

While Charless's newspaper was the third paper in Lexington, his establishment was the first bookstore in that city. The newspaper had a hard time succeeding. Charless formed a partnership first with Francis

Joseph Charless (1772–1834), an Irish immigrant printer and bookseller, was inexorably drawn to the frontier, establishing the first printing presses in Louisville, Kentucky, and in St. Louis, Missouri.

Joseph Charless Sr. Engraving. From the Collections of the St. Louis Mercantile Library at the University of Missouri–St. Louis.

Peniston, which dissolved only a few months later in May, and then with Robert Kay, which fell apart in September. At this point, Charless abandoned the paper to Kay (the *Gazetteer* folded six months later), because he had found that in Lexington bookselling was far more profitable than publishing the city's third newspaper. Charless even tried to sell his printing press and equipment but found no buyers.

The Irish bookseller discovered that people in the West were starved for books. He wrote to Mathew Carey on February 22, 1803:

> Classics has a great sale here. I could sell since I arrived some dozen of Virgils, Pantheons, Horace, Ovid &c &c. I had about 30 in all which are sold. Your Bibles are much wanted here if you could send me 50 cop. they could be sold … Religious books of almost every description are in demand. Particularly new authors ….

Charless also noted that he had an excellent market for scholarly books in Transylvania University (the oldest university west of the Alleghenies, founded in 1780): "The College here entirely depend on me for Scientific Books."

Carey's practice was to send Charless a mixture of the kinds of books he could readily sell and those that Carey had been unable to move in Philadelphia. This practice irked Charless, as books unlikely to sell in Philadelphia were equally unlikely to sell in Lexington, but the real tension between the two derived from Charless's seeming inability to pay Carey on time. As was already the case in Cincinnati during this period, the underlying problem was a lack of hard currency in the West. Charless wrote to Carey: "If you do not make up the orders and send them soon, I shall lose my credit with the people as a Bookseller. You will say quick remittance will cause the Books to travel post haste to Kentucky.—Believe me when I tell you I have not been able to collect the 1/6 of my Sales, and I am now determined to sell only by retail and for Cash (except Books of my own Printing)."

Nonetheless, Charless's Kentucky Printing Office & Bookstore was a

Mathew Carey was America's first modern publisher. A fugitive Irish activist and printer, he arrived aboard the ship *America* in Philadelphia in 1784. There over the next thirty years, he created the nation's foremost publishing house. Thoroughly committed to his new country, he always endeavored to help fellow Irish immigrants—one of whom was Joseph Charless—find a living in the book trade in the United States, particularly in the new settlements in the West. In doing so, he extended his own business as Charless and others penetrated into the frontier, carrying with them the Philadelphia publisher's books.

Mathew Carey (1760–1839). Prints and Photographs Division, Library of Congress (LC-USZ62-28998).

thriving operation that soon expanded into bookbinding as well. As he explained to Carey, "I can get here one Dollar per Quire Blank books (common kind). There are more work here than 3 binders could perform." By September 1803, Charless employed one journeyman binder and two apprentices.

His printing followed true to the frontier form. He issued an almanac, *Charless' Kentucky, Tennessee, & Ohio Almanac, for the Year of Our Lord 1804*, and his other publishing consisted of seven religious titles, four of which were commissioned by local churches. One of these religious titles was a hymnal specifically compiled for the western market. Charless initially printed 1,250 copies and sold them all immediately. He then printed a new edition of 2,000 copies. Charless could count on a good market for such books, but for other kinds of books, publication was a gamble. In such instances, a publisher was well advised to print up and circulate a prospectus to obtain advance subscriptions. Charless did just this for his 412-page edition of Jonathan Edwards's *Some Thoughts Concerning the Present Revival of Religion in New England*. On June 27, 1803, he told Carey that the work was being printed and that he had 1,567 advance subscriptions, which would have made for a print run of at

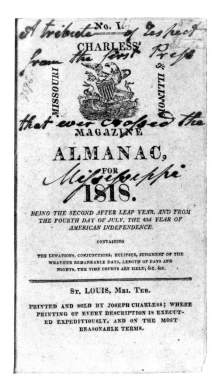

In 1817 Joseph Charless issued the first number of his *Missouri & Illinois Magazine Almanac*. Illustrated here is a presentation copy that is inscribed, "A tribute of respect from the first Press that ever crossed the Mississippi," quite possibly in Charless's own hand.

Title page from *Charless' Missouri & Illinois Magazine Almanac, for 1818*, no. 1 (St. Louis, Missouri Territory: Printed and sold by Joseph Charless, [1817]). Rare Book and Special Collections Division, Library of Congress.

least 2,000. This publishing pattern of almanacs, local religious texts, and an increasing number of schoolbooks continued for several years.

Bookselling, however, remained Charless's main source of income. In June 1804 he advertised for "A man of good character who will engage to carry Books through this state and Ohio, for sale. He can be furnished with a capital assortment of books and stationery, a cart, harness, &c." As Mathew Carey had discovered when he hired Mason Locke Weems (known popularly as Parson Weems) beginning in 1795 to peddle books in the countryside, there was a great deal of money to be made from book-starved readers in the more remote parts of the country. It was Charless's hope to find someone not unlike the extraordinarily successful Weems to beat the bushes in the West. We do not know if anyone answered the call, but it seems unlikely, because in 1805 Charless set out himself on a book-peddling expedition that took him through Ohio and the Indiana territory. He sold books to all kinds of people in towns, on farms, and along the roads, and he left quantities of books with local merchants on consignment, thus establishing a network of agents. It must have been a successful trip, because, as soon as he returned to Lexington, he loaded up the wagon again, this time entirely with schoolbooks, and set off south to Nashville, where he traded them all for bales of cotton.

At about the same time, however, Carey had decided that he was not being well treated by Charless. On April 13, 1805, he wrote Charless asking that he turn over all Carey's unsold books, particularly the Bibles, to the Lexington firm of Maccoun & Tilford, obtain a receipt for them, and pay the difference owed to Carey. Charless did not respond, and on July 12 Carey wrote again. Still Charless did not respond. Carey wrote yet again on August 15 and again on September 5. Finally on November 5, 1805, Charless answered that he had turned over Carey's books to Maccoun & Tilford, but as to those books he had already sold, "I would remit you for them but I really have no Money at present. Be assured Sir I will remit as soon as possible, but for old Acquaintance sake I hope you will be lenient." Carey replied on January 20, 1806, "You ought not to have appropriated the proceeds of my Bibles to any purpose whatever, but remitting me the amount as soon as it came into your possession."

Still Carey did not receive his money and on May 13 he wrote, "It is painful to me to observe that I think you use me very ill. I did not expect, nor had you any right, to keep me out of my money, to buy real estate, or to build." And indeed Charless had recently leased an important piece of real estate that included the Lexington town spring, and he was obviously playing fast and loose with Carey's money. We simply do not know, however, exactly what Charless was really trying to do, and in fact after only twenty months he traded away his lease, implying that his original scheme had not come to fruition.

Whatever Charless's successes and failures in Lexington may have been, by mid-1807 he was growing restless and turning his eyes westward. In this yearning for the West, he was like others in Kentucky. In 1826, Timothy Flint recalled his meeting with a restless Kentuckian some years before.

We purchased a Kentucky flat[boat], of forty tons . . . A few hours before sunset we went on board with a number of passengers, besides my family, and I introduced my family to the one that was already on board. He proved to be a fine, healthy-looking Kentuckian, with a young and pretty wife, two or three negro-servants, and two small children. He was a fair specimen of the rough and frank Kentucky character of men of his class; an independent farmer, who had swarmed from the old homestead hive in Kentucky. Land, there, he said, had already become too scarce and dear. He wanted elbow-room, did not wish to have a neighbor within three miles of him, and was moving to the upper Mississippi, for range.

In October 1807, Charless settled his affairs in Lexington and set out for the town of Louisville on the falls of the Ohio River, which he had first visited twelve years earlier. Here he established a new printing office to publish the *Louisville Gazette* and a bookstore, apparently enjoying moderate success.

A year before Charless's departure for Louisville, an event had occurred on the frontier that intensely focused the nation's attention on the West. In late September 1806, Meriwether Lewis and William Clark returned down the Missouri River to St. Louis, having crossed the continent and reached the Pacific Ocean in one of the most amazing journeys of exploration ever undertaken. Captain Lewis immediately wrote to President Jefferson to inform him of the expedition's return. William Clark wrote a similar letter to his family in Kentucky.

The nation learned of the expedition's success through a chain of newspapers. In the West, news traveled fastest as one newspaper picked up the story and then the next reprinted it. St. Louis had neither a printer nor a newspaper; the nearest was in Frankfort, Kentucky. The Frankfort *Western World* printed a copy of Captain Clark's letter on October 11, 1806, and Charless must have seen it very soon after, as it was reprinted in the Lexington papers. By October 28 the news had reached Pittsburgh, where it was printed in the *Gazette* on that date. On November 3, the news appeared in the Washington, D. C., *National Intelligencer*, where the members of Congress and the government first received word. Lewis's letter to Jefferson came into the president's hands on October 24, but Jefferson made no public comment until December 2, 1806.

With the return of Lewis and Clark, the importance of St. Louis to the nation as the gateway to the new territories in the West was magnified. The town had been named for King Louis IX by the French merchant and adventurer Pierre Laclède in 1764 when it was founded as a trading post on the west bank of the Mississippi River about nine miles south of its juncture with the Missouri River. Soon after, in 1770, the small French community came under Spanish control, but St. Louis retained its French character. The town thrived, in good part as a result of its exceptional location, and by 1774 it boasted a population of more than 650, which grew to more than 900 by 1799. In 1800 the French once again took possession, but soon after, in 1803, sold the whole of Louisiana to the United States. In March 1804 Captain Amos Stoddard formally took possession of St. Louis for the United States. And in May of that year Lewis and Clark set off from St. Louis on their epic journey of exploration.

St. Louis in 1808 was still very much a French city that respected its traditions of culture and civility; yet it was also a rough-and-tumble frontier town that had become invigorated with an American boomtown mentality. The town itself stretched along the bank of the river for about a mile and a half, its twelve mercantile establishments trading mostly in pelts, furs, and lead. French and American adventurers were swarming westward, where they encountered extraordinary opportunities for vast profit and equally great risks of abject ruin.

The authorities in St. Louis had felt the need for a press for some years. In 1808 the new governor of the territory, Meriwether Lewis, offered Joseph Charless financial assistance in moving from Louisville to St. Louis to set up shop. To reach Charless, Lewis wrote to his fellow expedition leader and great friend William Clark, then in the vicinity of Louisville, on May 29:

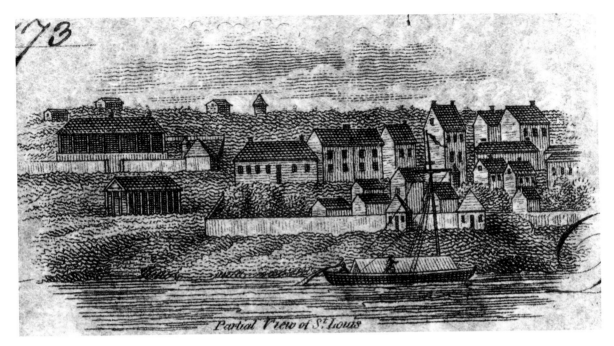

Partial View of St Louis

Inform Mr. Charless that I have made no arrangements with any other Printer [for] publishing the laws of the Territory, but that if he calculates on my encouragement and support he must come forward in person as soon as possible. The Legislature will meet on the second Monday in June to revise the laws of the Territory and will most probably originate others, a printer is absolutely necessary.

Within four weeks Charless was in St. Louis, but without a press. He had ordered a new Ramage press to be shipped down the Ohio River from Pennsylvania with all due dispatch, and now in St. Louis he was circulating the following prospectus, which he had printed in Louisville before his departure.

PROSPECTUS

It is self evident that in every country where the rays of the press is not clouded by despotic power, that the people have arrived to the highest grade of civilization, there science holds her head erect, and bids her sons to call into action close talents which lie in a good soil inviting cultivation. The inviolation of the Press is co-existent with the liberties of the people, they live or die together, it is the vestal fire upon the preservation of which, the fate of nations depends; and the most pure hands officiating for the whole community, should be incessantly employed in keeping it alive.

In 1808, when Joseph Charless established the first press west of the Mississippi River in this frontier settlement, St. Louis was still very much a French town. The arrival of a press was but one signal that the town was growing into a bustling American city. The earliest view of St. Louis, from a circulating note of the Bank of St. Louis in 1817, shows the city from the river.

Detail from a ten dollar bank note, Bank of St. Louis, 1817. Engraved by Leney and Rollinson, New York. Collection of Eric P. Newman Numismatic Education Society, St. Louis.

It is now proposed to establish a Weekly-Paper, to be published by subscription at St. Louis, to be called the

MISSOURI GAZETTE,

AND LOUISIANA ADVERTISER;

BY JOSEPH CHARLESS.

For the reasons above stated, we conceive it unnecessary to offer any thing like professions to the public, but rather let the columns of the GAZETTE speak for themselves, and the print let to live or die by the character it may acquire, but its intended Patrons have a right to be acquainted with the grounds upon which their approbation is solicited....

CONDITIONS

I. The Gazette will be published once a week on a handsome Type and Paper, the day of publication will be regulated by the arrival of the Mail; during the session of Congress, should their proceedings be particularly interesting, a supplementary sheet shall be occasionally issued.

The *Missouri Gazette*, established by Joseph Charless in 1808 in St. Louis, was much more than just a city newspaper. In its early years, it served a vast region, reaching readers across Missouri, Illinois, Indiana, Wisconsin, and further west. Charless intended that it should be nonpartisan and publish not only news, but also literary pieces and practical items that would advance the cause of civilization in the wilderness.

II. Terms of payment will be Three Dollars payable in advance, or Four Dollars in Country Produce. Advertisements not exceeding a square will be inserted one week for one dollar, and for every continuance Fifty Cents, those of a greater length in proportion.

Missouri Gazette, July 26, 1808. From the Collections of the St. Louis Mercantile Library at the University of Missouri–St. Louis.

The first Number of the Gazette, will appear as soon as possible, the Types being ready at Louisville, Ky. and the press expected in the course of a month, from Pennsylvania. The intended editor pledges his reputation, that there shall be no unnecessary delay.

The new printing press arrived on schedule, and with 174 subscriptions in hand, Charless set up shop in the Robidoux house on Main Street, between Pine and Spruce Streets. The first issue of the *Missouri Gazette*, the first newspaper printed in the trans-Mississippi West, was printed on July 12, 1808. Now at last St. Louis had a newspaper and a press.

Books had long been a part of the city's culture, and many leading citizens had private libraries. When Pierre Laclède died in 1778, he left a library of about two hundred volumes. But in 1808, St. Louis still lacked a bookstore. Many merchants sold a few books, such as Jacob Philipson who advertised in the *Gazette* in November 1808 that he had "a few German and English Bibles and Testaments, Hymn Books, etc., for sale." Nevertheless, Charless did not open a bookstore as he had done in other places in the past, and a separate book shop did not appear in St. Louis before 1820.

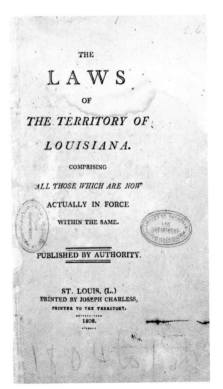

Charless spent a good part of the rest of 1808 in settling things in Kentucky and moving everything to Missouri. No doubt for Charless, the most important aspect of his new situation was that he was now publisher of the *Gazette*, a position of great prestige, but Meriwether Lewis probably quickly reminded him that he had accepted monetary support to come to St. Louis in order to print the territorial laws. And so in his capacity as public printer, Charless embarked on *The Laws of the Territory of Louisiana*, the first full book to be printed in the new territory. It was a long and arduous task, a book of more than four hundred pages, begun in July 1808 and finally finished in May 1809.

Though Joseph Charless continued as Printer to the Territory, it was as publisher and editor of the *Gazette* that he made his mark. The newspaper had no competition until 1815, but, even so, publishing a paper that served a vast region on a regular schedule was a daunting task. Like every frontier printer, Charless struggled with the problem of paper supply. It may be that he initially used locally made paper, but soon, in February 1809, he sent an order for a supply of large-sheet paper to the Jackson & Sharpless Papermill near Brownsville, Pennsylvania.

When the new paper failed to arrive before his current stock was exhausted, he was forced, like his contemporaries in Cincinnati and elsewhere, to print on smaller writing paper until the new shipment arrived. The War of 1812 exacerbated the supply problem and in mid-1812 Charless ran out of ink. By the end of 1813 he was faced with another paper shortage, and on December 11 he announced that "the Editor will be compelled to suspend publication of the *Gazette* for a few weeks." He explained that he had ordered and paid for ample quantities of paper in the East, "but in consequence of no regular trade being carried on with that place, his paper waits for an accidental trader coming this way." The paper finally made its way to St. Louis, and the *Gazette* resumed normal production on February 26, 1814.

Another challenge was getting up-to-date news. The news traveled by the U.S. mail, a most unreliable service in the West. This was owing in part to the fact that the U.S. Post Office contracted mail delivery to local agents, who were not always punctual or honest. Another factor was the nature of the environment itself. The mail had to be delivered in all seasons, across difficult terrain, and in the face of Indian or outlaw attacks. Charless had a particularly difficult time in the winter of 1808–9. After nine weeks without mail, he sent a man to Vincennes in the Indiana Territory to collect the mail there. When he returned with only a few pieces of mail, including newspapers over three months old, Charless was heartily disappointed, because it was from such newspapers that he obtained most of his news. Just as the news of Lewis and Clark's triumphal return had spread from newspaper to newspaper across the West, so too did every other kind of news get reprinted from paper to paper.

Perhaps the ultimate challenge was to get subscribers to pay. Of course, as we have seen in Cincinnati and elsewhere, this was not simply a matter of bad debts, but more often than not one of a lack of hard currency. Nonetheless, this was a perennial problem for the publisher, one never resolved. On April 19, 1810, Charless wrote, "The editor begs leave to inform those subscribers to the *Gazette* who are in arrears almost two years, that he is made of flesh and blood, that cameleon like he does not live on air, but endeavors to subsist like other folks." On July 20 he went further: "To those who have only lent us their names, we have to request them to give us a better evidence of their wish to support the first press

When Joseph Charless was invited by territorial governor Meriwether Lewis to set up the first printing press in St. Louis in 1808, it was for the purpose of printing the laws of the Louisiana Territory. For Charless, the invitation meant a chance to establish a newspaper, but he dutifully began work on the four-hundred-page book of laws in July 1808, the same month he launched his *Missouri Gazette*, finishing in May 1809.

Title page from *The Laws of the Territory of Louisiana, Comprising All Those Which Are Now in Force within the Same* (St. Louis: Joseph Charless, 1808 [actually 1809]). Law Library, Library of Congress.

that has yet ascended the Mississippi." Such pleas continued on a regular basis, and in 1816 he made his most eloquent appeal:

Could a printer strike sustenance from his head, as Vulcan struck Pallas from the head of Jove, then, indeed, it would be folly in him to complain; but such miracles are not to be worked now-a-days. Or could his look convert stones into flesh, as the head of Medusa did flesh into stone, he might do tolerably well. But printers unfortunately for themselves, are no magicians, altho' they deal in an art which has charmed mankind. They have much headwork to perform; but their teeth require to be occupied also. Indeed, with some, the occupation with the teeth is the major object. And, to confess the truth, it forms a part of our ambition also, otherwise we should not now be writing this paragraph.

In plain terms, we think ourselves full as competent to sign a receipt as write a paragraph. And we would thank those who wish us to perform the latter, to first call and take with them a specimen of the former—for like what the federalists used to say of Bonaparte, we "want money and must have it."

In spite of all these difficulties, the *Missouri Gazette* was a success. Beginning with 174 subscribers in 1808, the paper boasted about 500 in 1815 and a circulation that reached readers across Missouri, Illinois, Indiana, Wisconsin, and further west, which generated an annual income of about two thousand dollars. Advertising also increased at a similar rate and soon represented the publisher's largest source of steady income, bringing in about twenty-five hundred to three thousand dollars per annum.

Charless hoped that the *Gazette* would be more than a typical newspaper, particularly a partisan one. On January 4, 1809, he set out his vision for the newspaper:

I beg leave to request those gentlemen who promised literary aid, to collect such materials as may enrich its columns and render the Gazette worthy of general request.

Essays on morals and government, concise pieces on history (particularly the early settlement and progressive growth of Louisiana,) Antiquities, Topography, Botany, and vegetable Materia Medica, and Mineralogy, with such hints on husbandry as may tend to induce the Planter to embrace those wonderful advantages nature has thrown in his way. Indian manners and customs with their best speeches, Cases argued and determined in our Courts, or anything that may contribute to enliven the passing moment by an ingenious Tale or Song, will be gratefully received and carefully inserted.

For some years the *Gazette* and its readers fulfilled Charless's intention, and the newspaper functioned not only in the traditional mode of delivering news of the wider world but also as a reflection of the hopes, aspirations, and deeds of the citizens of St. Louis and the vast territories to the west. Charless did indeed print literary pieces and occasional poems by local poets. On December 12, 1810, he printed one such piece by Frederick Bates, "A Talk of the Big Soldier Delivered May 1807 in a Council Held with the Osages by Major Peter Chouteau." In that same issue he also printed extracts from Marshall's *History of Kentucky*. On February 14, 1811, Charless printed a review of Christian Schultz's *Travels on an Inland Voyage*, which had recently been published in New York and included a description of St. Louis from several years earlier. Contemporary accounts of the city and the surrounding territories came from the pen of Henry Marie Brackenridge in 1811, a series that was so well regarded that President Jefferson asked for a complete set. These essays were brought together and published in Pittsburgh in 1814 under the title *Views of Louisiana*. In 1812 the *Gazette* carried a series of articles on animal husbandry and agriculture, and in April 1814 it contained a biographical sketch of Matthew Elliott, who as British superintendent of Indian affairs in Canada was a figure of great interest to American merchants trading up the Missouri.

Charless's printing office came to resemble a reading room and became a regular stop for residents and itinerants alike who desired news. Because Charless received a large variety of newspapers from other places, there was always a good number of politicians, merchants, lawyers, soldiers, mountainmen, traders, trappers, keelboaters, and others gathered in his office sifting through the papers. In 1810, the Scots naturalist John Bradbury visited an Omaha village more than 500 miles up the Missouri River where two Indians told him of their visit to the *Gazette* office:

I had no recollection of these Indians, but they pointed down the river to St. Louis: afterwards they took up the corner of the buffalo robe, held it before their faces, and turned it over as a man does a newspaper in reading it. This action will be explained by relating that I frequented the printing-office of Mr. Joseph Charless, when at St. Louis, to read the papers from the United States, when it often happened that the Indians at that place on business came into the office and sat down. Mr. Charless, out of pleasantry, would hand to each a newspaper, which, out of respect for the custom of the whites, they examined with as much attention as

if they could read it, turning it over at the same time that they saw me turn that
with which I was engaged.

If Charless hoped to avoid partisan politics, he harbored a futile expec-
tation. The major controversy in the new territory centered on the legiti-
macy of Spanish land grants and pitted the old and established families—
who had such grants and were known as the Little Junto—against
newcomers—who wanted access to the lands and were known as anti-
Junto. Charless generally sided with the newcomers but always provided
space for opposing viewpoints. Still, the *Gazette* was identified with the
anti-Junto party in spite of Charless's protestations: "I must take this
opportunity to contradict a report industriously circulated that 'the
Gazette is under certain control.' I hereby declare the assertion to be false."

In 1814 he published an anonymous article, simply signed Q, which
severely criticized the military abilities of the former territorial governor,
General Benjamin Howard. Many, particularly the Little Junto supporters
of Howard, were sure Charless himself was Q. An armed group of them
entered the printing office one Sunday morning.

Before these men came to the office, they thought proper to denounce me as the
author of "Q" in the last week's *Gazette*, one said I was a liar, &c. This kind of
language was certainly not calculated to smooth the way to an amicable
ecclaireissement. No, the object was to control or destroy the liberty of the Press
in this place, or why should two judges of the court of common pleas armed with
a sword and a club, on a Sunday to enter rudely the Printing Office, and demand
in a dictatorial manner the author of "Q" in the last paper: This style could only
meet with the answer given; "I have been informed you have denounced me as the
author, therefore you shall have no satisfaction from me."

My patrons may rest assured, that I shall preserve the Liberty of the Press as
long as I am able to control one, and when I become the humble tool of factious
men, I shall no longer hope to merit support.

Not long after this incident, the Junto forces decided to establish a
competing newspaper. On April 16, 1814, they advertised in the Lexington
Reporter that "the people of St. Louis are desirous of procuring a printer
… a man of correct republican principles, with even moderate abilities
would satisfy." Charless reprinted the notice and responded: "It is a well
known fact, that the people of St. Louis, audaciously styled as above,
consist of only five or six individuals: and that the Editor of the *Missouri*

Gazette does meet with the decided approbation of the People of St. Louis, the *little* lawyer, and *would be* Lord Mayor, to the contrary notwithstanding." Still, the Junto persevered, and by early 1815 Joshua Norvell had been induced to leave the *Illinois Herald* of Kaskaskia for St. Louis. In June the *Western Journal* began publication. In it, accusations and denunciations were traded back and forth between Charless and William C. Carr, of the Junto. On July 21, Charless reported:

Yesterday evening, when I was conversing with some gentlemen near the post-office of St. Louis, William C. Carr approached close to me, without my observing him, and spit in my face, and at the same instant drew a pistol and presented it towards me. Being altogether unarmed, not even a stick in my hand, I had no other resort but stoning him, from which I was soon prevented by individuals, who interfered and laid hold of me, which gave Carr an opportunity of retreating to his house, no doubt exulting at his own *brave* and manly management of the affair, and at the strong proof he had given of his being a *gentleman* and a soldier.

Such confrontations continued and only heightened the political tension. But not all such attacks were politically motivated. The editor of any newspaper was in the public eye and might be held accountable for anything that appeared in print. In September 1817 a young man came to Charless and demanded to know the identity of the author of an anonymous letter on the upcoming elections in Kentucky. Charless refused to tell him.

Next day after breakfast, the young man appeared in the Office, with a dagger and sword cane, and demanded in a dictatorial manner the author of the letter—he was again informed he could not be gratified,—and after a pause of several minutes, he very modestly declared that, "as I was roughly handled here, he did not wish to have any difficulties with me!—and immediately on the back of this declaration, he said that the author and publisher of the letter, were d——d villains, &c." He was then ordered to walk out of the Office, and on his refusal, I accompanied him half way to the door, when he wheeled round and drew a dagger and sword cane, and made a pass at me & declared he "would be the instant death of me." In the interim, the young gentlemen, then in the office, got him out, and on my looking out at the door to see if he was gone, he threw a stone at my head, which I with difficulty evaded, and then, and not until then, (although reported otherwise) I fired at him. The pistol was some time charged—it hung fire—and I am happy to say, the life of an intemperate youth has been saved.

When Thomas Hart Benton arrived in St. Louis in 1815, he quickly joined the Junto, a group of powerful men opposed by Joseph Charless and his *Missouri Gazette*, and soon became its leader. In that same year, the Junto created a rival newspaper, the *Western Journal*, which was renamed the *Enquirer* in 1818 when Benton became its editor. The *Missouri Gazette* remained the region's dominant newspaper, but Benton made life unbearable for Charless, who finally gave up his press in 1820. As U.S. senator from Missouri, Benton went on to play a major role in national politics.

Thomas Hart Benton (1782–1858). Daguerreotype portrait photograph, by Mathew Brady's studio, ca. 1845–50. Prints and Photographs Division, Library of Congress (LC-USZ62-110024).

But all of these confrontations pale when compared to the troubles that arrived for Charless with Thomas Hart Benton in 1815. Colonel Benton, hero of the War of 1812, had fled Nashville after he and his brother Jesse wounded Andrew Jackson in a tavern brawl there. Now settled in St. Louis, Thomas Hart Benton was a commanding figure of great energy and presence, who immediately moved to become a leader of the Junto. Naturally he shared his new colleagues' intense dislike of Charless and the *Gazette*, an enmity that intensified when Benton killed Charless's close friend, Charles Lucas, in a duel soon after his arrival. Charless decried the affair in the *Gazette* at the time, and in a letter in 1819 would directly attack Benton's motives in the duel: "Mr. B. wishes to fill a senator's chair and will go through thick & thin to obtain it."

Benton was not a man to be trifled with, but he did not go after Charless quite yet, as indeed he had set his eye on "a senator's chair." The *Gazette* was still far and away the most successful newspaper in the region, and Charless could exert considerable influence on public opinion. The opposition *Western Journal* struggled to build circulation, changing its name three times and its editor nine times during its first ten years.

Obviously, only the will and subsidy of the Junto kept the paper afloat.

Then, in August 1818 an event occurred that must have alarmed Charless in the extreme. In that month Thomas Hart Benton became the editor of the Junto newspaper, which he renamed the *Enquirer*. Now Charless's greatest enemy was at the helm of a rival newspaper dedicated to destroying him. The two editors traded vitriolic barbs as the verbal war escalated, centering on the question of Missouri's proposed statehood. Benton and the Junto were proslavery advocates, whereas Charless held an antislavery position. The controversy was one of national importance, and the editorials of the two St. Louis papers were reprinted across the nation.

Charless published article after article opposed to slavery, and he even acted as chairman for public meetings in St. Louis, but when the election was finally held in May 1820, the proslavery forces achieved a decisive victory. The editor of the *Gazette* must have been crestfallen, but he responded, "We are contented. We never wish to interfere with the will of the people clearly and distinctly expressed."

Charless refused, however, to give up his disputes with Benton and his fellow editors, Isaac N. Henry and Evarist Maury, at the *Enquirer*. The *Enquirer* had criticized several ministers for supporting abolition, and Charless replied in the *Gazette*, "Is the right to engage in the discussion of the question of slavery and give an opinion upon it, really confined and secured to none but an old, sinful, obdurate bachelor, a father of negroes, and a murderer?" This was a direct personal attack on the three editors, and their response was swift.

The Editor of the Missouri *Gazette* whilst on the way from his office to his house, between one and two o'clock, on Wednesday the 10th of May . . . was assailed, as he ascended the hill, without any previous intimation, warning, or apparent quarrel, by Isaac N. Henry, one of the Editors of the St. Louis *Enquirer*, and receiving several blows with a heavy cudgel, which blows he returned with a stick disproportionately small; the combatants closed, fell, and struggled for a while. The Rev. Joseph Piggott, who was accompanying Mr. Charless, and was going to dine with him, twice endeavored to part them, but was as often prevented by a certain Wharton Rector, who drew a pistol from his bosom, and declared he would blow him through, if he interfered. Mr. Piggott then called for help, being determined to part them; presently two men came up and the contest ended.

Henry's attack on Charless became national news. The New York *Daily Advertiser* reported that Charless had been attacked by two young men whose combined ages did not equal the editor's fifty years and noted that "Mr. C. used the shilelah to great advantage, and when the battle ended, the amount of damage sustained fell upon Mr. Henry, whose shoulder was unjointed." Charless had attained a certain national prominence, but this merely heightened the conflict and made his enemies all the more determined.

Charless made the mistake of taking Henry to court. He won his case, but Benton, who knew the ins and outs of the courts and counted most of the judges as friends and fellow members of the Junto, then took Charless to court on a technicality and also won, sending Charless to jail for a time. Meanwhile Benton's political allies in the new legislature ensured that Henry received the contract to be the new state's official printer. Charless was never even invited to submit a bid. (In fact he did submit an unofficial bid far under that of Henry's, but it was ignored.)

It was all too much for the embattled and embittered editor of the *Gazette*, who announced his retirement on September 13, 1820. He sold the newspaper and the entire printing office. With this act, Joseph Charless removed himself from the book trade, but not from commercial life in St. Louis. He operated a boardinghouse and livery stable out of his home, and together with his son, Joseph, established a thriving business in the drug trade. He died a prosperous and respected citizen of St. Louis on July 28, 1834.

By the 1830s, St. Louis, like Cincinnati, could no longer be considered a frontier city. The frontier had moved westward and northward, where it had come up against both a natural barrier in the ever more arid lands of the Great Plains and an administrative barrier established by the federal government to protect the Indians. Though many traders and adventurers penetrated these barriers with little difficulty, immigrants looking for traditional homesteads turned south to Texas.

IN 1835 in Bath, New York, not far from Canandaigua, where J. D. Bemis had made his mark thirty years earlier and where he would live on until 1857, the news was all about revolution in Texas. Interest in the Texas frontier had been stimulated for some years by emigrant guidebooks, such as David Woodman's *Guide to Texas Emigrants* and Charles Edwards's *Texas and Coahuila*, which described Texas in glowing terms. We can imagine three young men, two brothers, Jacob Cruger and James Cruger, and Francis Moore Jr., poring over such guides and, as the news intensified,

In the mid-1830s the news was all about Texas. Paeans to the fertility of the boundless land just waiting to be claimed appeared juxtaposed in newspaper columns with descriptions of the outrages Mexicans committed against peaceful American emigrants. As events built toward revolution, guidebooks such as David Woodman's *Guide to Texas Emigrants*, published in Boston in 1835, provided useful information for the streams of Americans headed for Texas.

Title page from David Woodman Jr., *Guide to Texas Emigrants* (Boston: Printed by M. Hawes, for the Publishers, 1835). Rare Book and Special Collections Division, Library of Congress.

deciding to set off for Texas, to fight for freedom and become a part of this new and exciting frontier. By the spring of 1836 the three were in Cincinnati. Upon their arrival, they discovered that Captain James L. Allen was organizing a company of volunteers, the Buckeye Rangers, to aid the Texans. At the same time, Texan Gail Borden (who was later to make a fortune in the milk business) was in Cincinnati to buy a new press. Printer of the *Telegraph and Texas Register*, Borden published the official organ of the provisional government in San Felipe de Austin. When the Texans retreated from San Felipe, his press had been moved to safety in Harris-

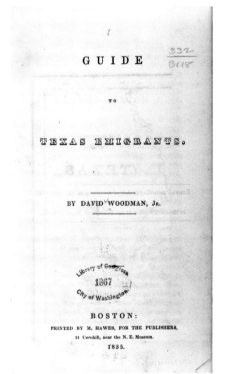

burg on Buffalo Bayou, but Santa Anna's troops had captured Borden and thrown his press into the bayou just days before the victory at San Jacinto on April 21. While Borden was in Cincinnati, it is quite possible that he met the three New Yorkers. But in any case, the trio joined the Buckeye Rangers, who soon boarded the steamboat *Farmer* bound for New Orleans, with connections to Texas.

The Cruger brothers and Moore arrived in Texas too late to participate in the crucial battles, but nonetheless they joined the Army of the Republic. Discharged on September 22, 1836, Jacob Cruger found work as a clerk in the War Department, and Moore served as an assistant surgeon. Soon, however, all three were literally knee-deep in the mud of the new town of Houston, where the two brothers set up in the merchandising business. Soon Jacob grew tired of trade and found work on Borden's newspaper, which had been relocated to Houston from San Felipe de Austin. On March 9, 1837, Moore bought part of the newspaper, and on June 20, Jacob Cruger bought the remaining portion from Borden. With the issue of June 24, 1837, the publishing firm of Cruger and Moore was launched.

Although printing had come to Texas as early as 1817, it had become an established business there only in 1829. The *Telegraph and Texas Register* was founded in October 1835, and it was, because of its close connection to the government, the most influential and widely read newspaper in Texas. After only a year, Cruger and Moore found themselves in possession of the new republic's most prestigious and influential press.

However prestigious Houston may have seemed from afar, the reality in the new city was mundane. "Mudtown," as the new city was known, was laid out on the edge of a prairie on the south side of Buffalo Bayou, a dynamic collection of tents, shanties, and log cabins, all being set up at a fantastic rate. A great sense of energy and enterprise was generated as the city rose out of the dirt, soon to be the capital city of the new republic. Streets were laid out and lots sold, as immigrants streamed in and churned up the mud. Housed in a small shack on Prairie Street the *Telegraph* was plagued by a roof that leaked. When the roof partially collapsed, it caused no little damage, as reported in the newspaper:

We have been deceived: no building had ever been nearly finished at Houston intended for the press; fortunately, however, we have succeeded in renting a shanty, which, although like the *capitol* in this place,

> *"Without a roof, and without a floor,*
> *Without windows and without a door,"*

is the only convenient building obtainable. . . .

Our troubles have not yet ended, the shanty is falling about our ears, two massive beams have dropped down upon the stands, made a most disgusting *pi* [spilled type], and driven the workmen to seek safety outside, the *devil* alone looks smiling on the mischief.

Like Charless's *Gazette* office in St. Louis, the *Telegraph* office served as a central meeting place and source for information. It was often one of the first stops for new immigrants interested in purchasing property or looking for employment. Of course copies of newspapers from across the country were available for perusal, and naturally the office became a gathering place for those interested in news and events. For a time the office even featured a pet bear, but its days were numbered after it attempted to assist with the press and dumped all the type on the floor, causing a serious delay in the paper's schedule.

A number of prominent citizens of the new city established the Philosophical Society of Texas in 1837 with the hope of eventually establishing a library in Houston. Other groups and organizations also worked to create a library in the early years, and finally in 1854, the Houston Lyceum was established at the initiative of Andrew Daly.

The *Telegraph and Texas Register* was issued weekly at a subscription price of five dollars per year, payable in advance. It continued to publish official documents and government proclamations, in addition to all the normal kinds of reports, articles, letters, and advertisements found in

The *Telegraph and Texas Register* was founded in 1835 at San Felipe de Austin by Joseph Baker and brothers Gail Borden and Thomas H. Borden. It served as the official newspaper for the provisional government, a role it was to maintain for many years to come. In 1837 Jacob Cruger and Francis Moore Jr. purchased the newspaper, established the firm of Cruger and Moore in Houston, and published the *Telegraph and Texas Register* there until, in 1851, Cruger sold out to Moore. During those years the newspaper was a strong advocate for statehood and on March 4, 1846, it proclaimed annexation as the font of the "future glory" of Texas.

Masthead, March 11, 1846, *Telegraph and Texas Register,* Houston. Courtesy of the American Antiquarian Society.

every newspaper across the country. Moore edited the paper, and Cruger managed the production. Like most newspapers of its day, the *Telegraph* was partisan and attacked such evils as dueling, gambling, drinking, and gunfighting, coming down especially hard on President Sam Houston and government corruption. In 1845 Houston said of Moore, who had lost an arm when young, "The lying scribbler of the *Telegraph*, is a one armed man. You never would forgive me for abusing a cripple, but I must confess that one arm can write more malicious falsehoods than any man with two arms I ever saw." Obviously Moore's editorials had found their mark. Issues of government corruption aside, the paper's overriding aim was to promote annexation with the United States, and for nine years Moore and Cruger tirelessly pushed for Texas to join the Union. And so it was with great jubilation and satisfaction that on March 4, 1846, the *Telegraph* was able finally to trumpet annexation as an accomplished fact.

Cruger and Moore published considerably more than the *Telegraph*. Not only did the firm do all kinds of job printing, such as handbills, land and stock certificates, warrants, letters of citizenship, and many different kinds of forms, but more significantly it served as public printer, first to the republic and then to the state. Established by Borden in October, 1836, this relationship was inherited by Cruger and Moore. The *Declaration of Independence Made at Washington on the Second of March, 1836, and the Constitution of the Republic of Texas Adopted by the Convention, March 17, 1836* (1837; 1838), the *Laws of the Republic of*

Texas in Two Volumes (1838), and the *Journals of the Consultation Held at San Felipe* (1838), among many other documents, were issued from the *Telegraph* office.

About a year after Cruger and Moore assumed the responsibilities of public printer, they were accused by J. Warren Niles, publisher of the *National Banner*, of overcharging the government, billing $8,640 for work Niles would have done for $2,652. Cruger and Moore replied that the contract had been negotiated by their predecessors at a time when the currency was worth about 25 percent of face value. They further explained that they had presented a much reduced bill to the secretary of state for the second volume of the laws, and because that bill was not for the original sum, it had been refused. After this Cruger and Moore continued to print government publications, but without pay for a period so as not to lose the contract.

And what has been the result? to have been first blamed because we were too poor to procure the means of publishing all the laws and journals of Congress, as expeditiously as they would have been published in the United States. And then to be taunted by one who has been laboring incessantly to "slip into our shoes," that we have "battened on the government"!! ... Whatever have been our transactions with government, they have been open and fair. ... But when men secretly sneak in, like "rats," to undermine our business and sustained by the means of our enemies, offer to do work lower than actual cost, in order that they may at some after period, ... raise their prices at pleasure; when such men oppose us, and ... intoxicated with that importance which the lackey feels, in a new livery, snap their fingers and say, "go poor devil, there is room enough in the world for me and thee," we shall say to them, go back ... to "your Masters, and learn better manners." ... We fight under the *Telegraph*, which has never been soiled by a base sentiment, and which has once passed through the fiery ordeal of Tyranny. We bid eternal defiance to the groveling reptiles who have leagued against us.

Public printing was important to the firm, so when the government moved the capital to Austin in 1839, Jacob Cruger went along. Moore remained in Houston and continued to publish the *Telegraph*. In

Jacob Cruger (d. 1864) and Francis Moore (1808–1864) formed an effective team in creating the publishing firm of Cruger and Moore in early Houston. Cruger handled the printing side and Moore the editorial.

Jacob W. Cruger, from Dudley G. Wooten, editor, *A Comprehensive History of Texas, 1685 to 1897*, 2 vols. (Dallas: William G. Scarff, 1898), 2:375. Library of Congress (Microfilm 36841 F).

Dr. Francis Moore, who lost an arm at an early age, studied medicine and law and began his Texas career as a surgeon, but he soon moved into the newspaper publishing business with his friend Jacob Cruger.

Dr. Francis Moore Jr., from Dudley G. Wooten, editor, *A Comprehensive History of Texas, 1685 to 1897*, 2 vols. (Dallas: William G. Scarff, 1898), 2:374. Library of Congress (Microfilm 36841 F).

addition, the firm had established a daily newspaper in Houston, the *Morning Star*. This paper was printed in the *Telegraph* office on the old press that the Mexicans had thrown in the bayou, which had subsequently been rescued and refurbished. After Cruger left, the *Morning Star* was transferred to his brother James.

In Austin, Jacob Cruger not only continued as public printer but also founded the *Texas Centinel*. Cruger was successful in obtaining new contracts for public printing, in part, because he had "a large, Machine Power Press, which diminishes, in a great degree, the expense of the press work." A whole series of reports and documents was issued from the *Centinel* office in Austin, but as a result of both Indian and Mexican attacks on the town, the government returned to Houston in 1842. With the departure of the government, Cruger closed up the *Centinel* office and returned to the *Telegraph* office in Houston.

For Texas, 1845 was a momentous year. It was now clear, with the passage of a congressional resolution on March 1, that the United States was willing to annex Texas, and so a convention was called at Austin on July 4 to establish a constitution for the new state. Francis Moore Jr., who had served as Houston's first mayor and then as senator, was a participant and signer. Jacob Cruger served as printer to the convention and issued a special newspaper, the *New Era*, during the convention. In due course, Cruger printed the *Journals of the Convention* and the *Constitution*. Soon, however, he returned to Houston, where he managed to continue as public printer.

Houston in 1845 was no longer the rough-and-tumble Mudtown it had been when Cruger and Moore first set up the *Telegraph* office in 1837. It was an established and flourishing city with all the attributes and amenities of Cincinnati or St. Louis. It too had outgrown its status as a frontier town. Cruger sold his share of the *Telegraph* to Moore in 1851, and at that time the *Morning Star* was discontinued. Moore sold the paper three years later. When the Civil War came to Texas, Moore left for the North, where he died from injuries in 1864. Jacob Cruger joined the Confederate Army and died of illness in the same year. But the *Telegraph*, which had been at the center of the lives of the two men and of Texas alike, survived the war and continued until 1877.

THE ALPHABET.

39

VOWELS.		SOUND.	
Names.		Ex. in Eng.	Ex. in Hawaii.
A a	--- â	as in *father*,	la—sun.
E e	--- a	— *tete*,	hemo—cast off.
I i	--- e	— *marine*,	maric—quiet.
O o	--- o	— *over*,	ono—sweet.
U u	--- oo	— *rule*,	nui—large.

CONSONANTS.	Names.	CONSONANTS.	Names.
B b	be	N n	nu
D d	de	P p	pi
H h	he	R r	ro
K k	ke	T t	ti
L l	la	V v	vi
M m	mu	W w	we

The following are used in spelling foreign words.

| F f | fe | S s | se |
| G g | ge | Y y | yi |

1

Hawaii's first printer was a former journeyman trained by James Bemis in Canandaigua, New York. Elisha Loomis arrived in Hawaii in 1820 as a member of a missionary party. The press he brought with him was intended to print missionary tracts and schoolbooks in the Hawaiian language, but no printing could go forward until a written form of the language was devised. The first impression was pulled at a special ceremony held in Honolulu on January 7, 1822, when a single sheet, titled "Lesson I," the beginning of a primer in the Hawaiian language, was printed. Soon after, Loomis printed the full primer in 500 copies. In September, a second edition of 2,000 copies was issued, the initial page of which is illustrated here.

"The Alphabet," first page of a [*Primer of the Hawaiian Language*], 2nd ed. ([Honolulu: Elisha Loomis, September 1822]). Rare Book and Special Collections Division, Library of Congress.

CHAPTER THREE

ACROSS THE GREAT AMERICAN DESERT

In looking behind over the road just traveled, ... or forward over that to be taken, for an indefinite number of miles there seemed to be an unending stream of emigrant trains ... It was a sight which, once seen, can never be forgotten; it seemed as if the whole family of man had set its face westward.

—William G. Johnston, 1849

WELL BEFORE Texas entered the Union, the frontier had slowed its western movement. Many emigrants were unwilling to farm the treeless prairies, believing that heavily wooded land was a necessary mark of fertility. Then, too, they lacked the heavy plows and implements needed to break up the dense prairie sod. Nature herself defined a boundary, at about the ninety-eighth meridian—a north-south line about fifty miles west of Wichita, Kansas, and Oklahoma City, Oklahoma—beyond which the arid conditions made traditional farming nearly impossible. The animosity of the Plains Indians and the federal government's Indian policies of relocation and isolation in the 1830s created a barrier at about the ninety-fifth meridian, a north-south line at the western border of Missouri. To the west was Indian Territory, which was strictly forbidden to white settlement, whose border was aggressively patrolled by the army. This vast region encompassing the Great Plains was known as the Great American Desert, "those barren wastes, the haunts of the buffalo and the Indian." As Francis Parkman described it in 1846, a place "where the very shadow of civilization lies a hundred leagues behind."

The 1830s were a time of massive European emigration, causing the pressure for new land to continue to build. From the 1820s, Texas had offered an alternative destination, but it remained Mexican territory until 1836 and an independent nation until 1845. To the north, Wisconsin and

Minnesota presented land and opportunities for settlers, but these outlets were insufficient to satisfy the ever-growing demand. A few intrepid settlers had made the arduous journey of two thousand miles across the vast plains and mountains to the Willamette Valley in Oregon, stimulated by the exertions and propaganda of Hall Jackson Kelley and his American Society for Encouraging the Settlement of the Oregon Territory during the late 1820s and early 1830s.

A simultaneous call for missionaries also focused attention on Oregon. Books had always been a part of the missionary experience, and the Bible was at the center of the proselytizing enterprise. Missions needed many other books as schools were established, and through missionary efforts, reading became a part of life for many indigenous peoples. Some missions even established their own printing presses to print the Bible and other works in the Indian languages.

Some of the first American missionaries in the West, sponsored by the American Board of Commissioners of Foreign Missions, set out from Boston and landed in Hawaii in 1820, having sailed around Cape Horn. One of their number was a printer, Elisha Loomis, who had been one of James Bemis's many apprentices in Canandaigua, New York. Loomis brought with him a printing press and all its equipment, with the intention of printing in the Hawaiian language. Before printing could proceed, the missionaries had to devise a written version of the Hawaiian language, a process that took some time. By late 1822, however, Loomis began to turn out works in the newly devised Hawaiian alphabet.

The Indians early on recognized the power of the book, particularly the "black book" carried by missionaries and priests. And they were also impressed with the ability possessed by the whites of communicating with one another over great distances by writing on paper. In 1831, four Indians—three Nez Percés and a Flathead—appeared in St. Louis hoping to find someone who would bring the "black book" to their peoples and reveal its powerful mysteries. They spoke to William Clark—the great explorer who was now commissioner for Indian affairs—and several priests. Only one Indian made it back home, two having died in St. Louis and one on the return trail, and he arrived without either a missionary or the "black book." Nevertheless, the presence in St. Louis of these four Indians was the subject of a letter written by William Walker, a Methodist Wyandot Indian, to a friend in the East. Walker's letter, which was rewritten and considerably exaggerated, was published in the *Christian*

Advocate and Journal, where the editor commented: "Hear! Hear! Who will respond to the call beyond the Rocky Mountains? ... We are for having a mission established there at once. ... All we want is men. Who will go? Who?"

When the call came for missionaries for the Oregon region, it was answered by Marcus Whitman. He spent 1835 exploring with fur trappers in the Rocky Mountains, where he concluded that there was much work to be done, and returned East to organize a mission. Joining Whitman was Henry Spalding, and with their new wives—all missionaries were required to be married—they headed west in 1836. The two young wives were the first white women to make the overland trek, and their appearance caused quite a sensation among the Indians and trappers along the route. The Whitmans and the Spaldings fell out during the journey—perhaps the fact that Narcissa Whitman had earlier rejected Spalding's proposal of marriage had something to do with the dispute—so each couple established a separate mission.

The Whitmans settled in Waiilatpu on the Walla Walla River, in what is now Washington State, and the Spaldings settled in Lapwai, on the Clearwater Fork of the Snake River in the country of the Nez Percé, in what is now Idaho. In the spring of 1839, the American Board of Commissioners of Foreign Missions decided to send Edwin Hall and his wife from Hawaii to the Lapwai mission. Hall had arrived in Hawaii in 1835 with a small Ramage tabletop printing press and its equipment, and it was in his capacity as printer that he was to serve in Lapwai. As had been true in Hawaii, it was necessary to create a written version of the local language before any printing could begin. Before leaving for Oregon, Hall wrote in his journal:

Mr. Spaulding has sent me a small elementary book in the Nez-Perces language in order that I could see the proportions of the various letters in putting up the type. He says also, that he shall this winter prepare some others, so that they will be ready for me to print when I arrive. I have accordingly put up our old fount of Pica and Long Primer English, and also the new fount of English, received within a year ago. The two former are nearly worn out; but the latter is almost new, but a small fount, being all contained in one case. The latter we can dispense with, with some inconvenience; and the two former are supplied with new founts recently received. The Press designed to be taken is only a small hand-card-press, which was a donation to this Mission, and came out with us in the [ship] *Helle-*

spont. I have had it put in order, by adding a frisket, points, etc, and hope to make it answer the purpose till the wants of those missions shall require greater facilities for the prosecution of that branch of labor. The type, also, will probably do till the language is so far reduced to system that the proper proportions can be sent for all of the letters. This will be done in the course of a year or two.

In April 1839, Mr. and Mrs. Hall reached Fort Vancouver on the Columbia River. They continued upstream to Fort Walla Walla, where they rested for a week, continuing up the Snake River to Lapwai on May 14. By May 16, Edwin Hall had the press set up and operational. On May 18, he pulled the first proof, and by May 24, he had produced 400 copies of an eight-page primer, entitled the *Nez-Percés First Book*. Hall and Spalding were very pleased with their labors, but as they examined the small booklet they discovered many errors. Spalding's alphabetic system was deficient and needed to be revised. The men concluded that this first product of the press should be destroyed and redone, and indeed no complete copies are known to have survived. Five hundred copies of a second version of the primer, now consisting of twenty pages, were completed in August.

In September, the Halls left Lapwai for Waiilatpu, the Whitmans' mission, where Mrs. Hall gave birth to a daughter in November. Hall had tried to have the press moved, but the pack animal carrying it fell over a cliff. The press was rescued and returned to Lapwai. Hall, whose wife was ill, returned to Lapwai briefly in January to work on a Nez Percé reader prepared by two other missionaries, A. B. Smith and Cornelius Rogers of the Kamiah mission. Hall worked on the reader for only one week and then left Lapwai, leaving Rogers to finish the book, which was published in February 1840. Obviously not happy with the situation at Lapwai, Hall never went back. Perhaps he shared Whitman's antipathy for Spalding. In any case, he and his family returned to Hawaii in May 1840.

The Lapwai press stood unused for two years. But in the fall of 1842 another book, of sixteen pages, was produced. Spalding reported: "Mr. Walker arrived the last of Nov. & with my poor

The first book printed in what is now Idaho was *Nez-Percés First Book: Designed for Children and New Beginners.* This missionary primer was written by Henry Spalding and printed on the Ramage press that Edwin Hall brought with him from Hawaii to the Lapwai mission in 1839.

Title page from Henry Harmon Spalding, *Nez-Percés First Book: Designed for Children and New Beginners,* 2nd version ([Lapwai mission station (Idaho): Edwin Oscar Hall, August 1839]). Rare Book and Special Collections Division, Library of Congress.

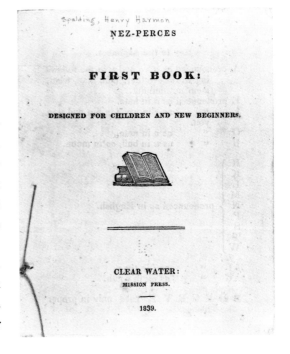

A Scottish immigrant, Adam Ramage (1771/72–1850) began manufacturing printing presses in Philadelphia in about 1800. He soon developed a small wooden press that was a favorite of frontier printers because of its portability. The press that was transported down the Ohio River to St. Louis for Joseph Charless in 1808 may well have been an early Ramage, as was the first printing press in New Mexico, which was taken over the Santa Fe Trail in 1834. Likewise, the first press in California was a Ramage press transported to Monterey that same year. Adam Ramage also made a small all-iron table press, one of which was used at the Lapwai mission in Idaho in 1839. Illustrated here, the Lapwai press was taken by missionaries from Boston to Hawaii to the West Coast and then up the Columbia and Snake Rivers to the Lapwai mission.

Photograph of the Lapwai Mission Press. Courtesy of the Oregon Historical Society (OrHi 26237).

assistance fitted up the press & printed a small book in the Flat-Head language." Walker continued in his own report:

Since you were last written to from this station a small book of sixteen pages has been printed in the native language. The type was mostly set by myself. The printing of this book detained me at Clear Water about eleven days. You will readily suppose that it was slow work as it was wholly new business both to Mr. Spalding and myself. Mr. S. understood working the press as it had been taken down and laid aside since Mr. Hall left the country. Among the most difficult things to be done was the making of a new roller which we succeeded in after three or four attempts. We not only succeeded in making one but we made a good one.

After Walker's departure, Spalding continued to work with the press and to print first an eight-page booklet of Nez Percé laws and then a thirty-six-page hymn book.

After this burst of activity, the press was not again used until 1844, when a printer, Medare G. Foisy, appeared in Lapwai. Foisy had been brought up in the trade in Canada and had worked in Cincinnati, Louisville, and St. Louis before going west. He remained for one year in Lapwai, where he printed a Nez Percé translation of the Gospel of Matthew and an English-Nez Percé vocabulary. This was the end of printing at Lapwai.

Foisy left for Oregon, where he did a little printing with type owned by the Catholic mission in St. Paul in 1845 (apparently without a press), and then he traveled on to Monterey, California, where he printed the pioneer newspaper, the *Californian*, in 1846. The Lapwai press itself was successfully moved to Waiilatpu and was there when the Cayuse Indians attacked the mission in 1847, killing the Whitmans and a dozen other settlers. The

The California Job Case has long been associated in the popular imagination with the gold rush and the overland movement. The printers who accompanied these pioneers reportedly rejected the traditional use of two separate cases for each font (an upper case for capital letters and a lower case for the small letters) and instead combined a whole font in a single case, which came to be known as the California Job Case. Combined cases were available for sale by the 1830s, and no doubt pioneer printers used these cases to make the transportation of type more efficient. But the California Job Case, specifically identified as such, was not introduced until 1876, when O. A. Dearing of the Printers' Furnishings Warehouse in San Francisco first announced its availability in *Type and Graver*.

"California Job Case," from Barnhart Bros. & Spindler, *Book of Type Specimens* (Chicago: Barnhart Bros. & Spindler, [1907]). General Collections, Library of Congress.

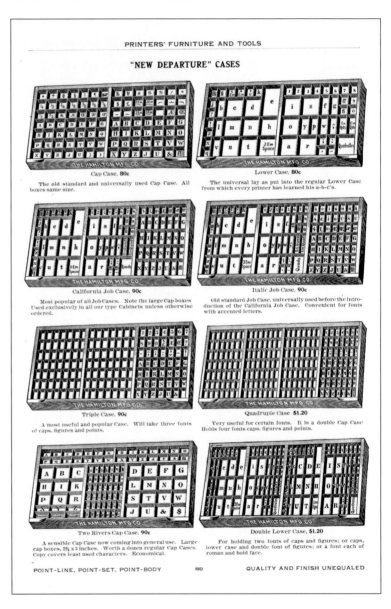

PRINTERS' FURNITURE AND TOOLS

"NEW DEPARTURE" CASES

Cap Case, 80c
The old standard and universally used Cap Case. All boxes same size.

Lower Case, 80c
The universal lay as put into the regular Lower Case from which every printer has learned his a-b-c's.

California Job Case, 90c
Most popular of all Job Cases. Note the large Cap boxes Used exclusively in all our type Cabinets unless otherwise ordered.

Italic Job Case, 90c
Old standard Job Case, universally used before the introduction of the California Job Case. Convenient for fonts with accented letters.

Triple Case, 90c
A most useful and popular Case. Will take three fonts of caps, figures and points.

Quadruple Case, $1.20
Very useful for certain fonts. It is a double Cap Case Holds four fonts caps, figures and points.

Two Rivers Cap Case, 90c
A sensible Cap Case now coming into general use. Large cap boxes, 2¾ x 3 inches. Worth a dozen regular Cap Cases. Copy covers least used characters. Economical.

Double Lower Case, $1.20
For holding two fonts of caps and figures; or caps, lower case and double font of figures; or a font each of roman and bold face.

POINT-LINE. POINT-SET. POINT-BODY   889   QUALITY AND FINISH UNEQUALED

Jotham Meeker (1804–1855) was a Baptist missionary printer. Having learned his trade in Cincinnati, he arrived in the Indian Territory at the Shawanoe mission station in March 1834, in what is now the state of Kansas. One of the first books to issue from the press was Isaac McCoy's *Annual Register of Indian Affairs*. McCoy (1784–1846), too, was a Baptist missionary, who also served as an Indian agent. Meeker began work on the book on December 15, 1834, and finished on January 17, 1835. He wrote in his journal, "Finish Br. M'Coy's Ann. Reg. a work of 52 pages, including the Cover. 1000 copies." McCoy said of the book, "I published it at my own cost, and circulated it gratuitously. One was sent to each member of Congress, and to each principal man in the executive departments of Government."

Annual Register of Indian Affairs within the Indian (or Western) Territory, no. 1 (Shawanoe Mission: Jotham Meeker, printer, 1835). Rare Book and Special Collections Division, Library of Congress.

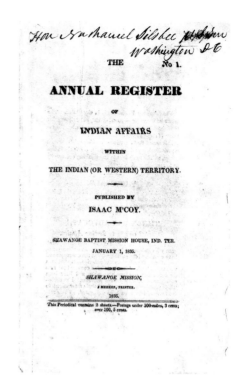

press eventually found its way to the Oregon Historical Society in Portland, where it has been preserved to this day.

Elsewhere in the Indian Territory, missionaries, like their brethren at Lapwai, were introducing printing presses, books, and literacy to new regions and peoples. At the Shawanoe mission in what is now Kansas, Jotham Meeker, who had learned his trade in Cincinnati, set up a press in 1834. In the first book to issue from the press, *The Annual Register of Indian Affairs within the Indian (or Western) Territory*, its publisher, Isaac McCoy, noted:

At the Shawanoe station is a printing press in operation, under the management of Jotham Meeker, Missionary for the Ottawas. Mr. Meeker has invented a plan of writing . . . by which, Indians of any tribe may learn to read in their own language in a few days. The first experiment was made with a sprightly Chippewa boy, wholly ignorant of letters, and of the English language. He studied three hours each day for nine days; at the expiration of which time there was put into his hands a writing of about twenty lines, of the contents of which he had no knowledge. After looking over it a few minutes, without the aid of an instructer [*sic*], the boy read off the writing, to the unspeakable satisfaction of the teacher. Upon this plan elementary school books have been prepared, and printed, viz. – In Delaware, two; in Shawanoe, two; in Putawatomie, one; and two in Otoe, besides a considerable number of Hymns, &c. The design succeeds well.

As the displaced Cherokee Nation found a new home to the south in what is now Oklahoma, so too did the printer John Fisher Wheeler make a home there. Wheeler had been head printer of the Cherokee Press in New Echota in Georgia. The Cherokees—and the Chickasaws, Choctaws, Creeks, and to some degree the Seminoles—had embraced European ways decades before. They had made great strides in agriculture and animal husbandry and had established self-government and small industries such as flour mills and cotton spinning. They even had their own written alphabet, created by Sequoyah, who with no knowledge of written English or any other European language had devised the Cherokee alphabet (or more properly a syllabary), which he called his "talking leaves." Based on Sequoyah's alphabet, the Cherokees created a printing house, which produced a newspaper and such works as the Bible translated into Cherokee. Soon almost two-thirds of the population was literate.

Nonetheless, the Cherokee Nation was forced out of Georgia along the "trail of tears" to the Indian Territory, where they were reunited with a smaller group that had moved west decades earlier. It was under these

The third item to be printed at the Union Mission Station on the Grand River in present-day Oklahoma was John Fleming's *Istutsi in naktsokv; or, The Child's Book*. Printed by John Fisher Wheeler before October 31, 1835, the book consisted of twenty-four pages in an edition of 500 copies. The primer is in the Creek language, represented in the Pickering alphabet, and uses woodcut illustrations. James Perryman, a Creek Indian, assisted in the translation.

Istutsi in naktsokv; or, The Child's Book, by Rev. John Fleming, Missionary of the American Board of Commissioners for Foreign Missions (Union Mission Station on the Grand River [Oklahoma]: John Fisher Wheeler, printer, 1835), 4–5. Rare Book and Special Collections Division, Library of Congress.

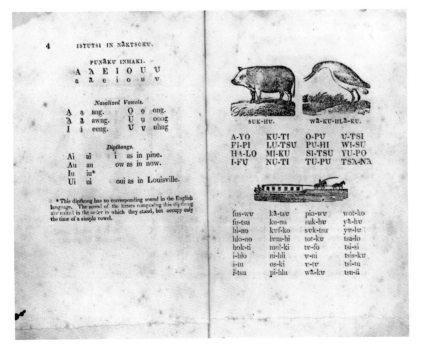

The first printing in what is now Wyoming (then part of the Utah Territory) occurred at Fort Bridger in 1863. This was a post newspaper, the *Daily Telegraph,* which appeared during June and July of that year. The first permanent press was established in Cheyenne in September 1867 to publish the *Cheyenne Leader*. Joseph Gebow's *Vocabulary of the Snake, or, Sho-Sho-Nay Dialect*, illustrated here, was published by a peripatetic press operated by the Freeman brothers. The Freemans had purchased the press used to print the *Herald* at Fort Kearney in Nebraska. As the Union Pacific Railroad moved westward, the Freeman brothers moved the press along the same route. In 1868, they stopped with their press for two months in Green River, where they printed Gebow's *Vocabulary of the Snake*.

Page from Joseph A. Gebow, *A Vocabulary of the Snake or Sho-Sho-Nay Dialect* (Green River City, Wyoming Territory: Freeman & Bro., Printers, 1868). Rare Book and Special Collections Division, Library of Congress.

A VOCABULARY

OF THE

SNAKE OR SHO-SHO-NAY DIALECT

A

A tin cup,	Augoots.
All of you,	Himoyeant.
A sword,	Kivarant wit.
All gone,	Mat-so mahgan.
A gun sight,	Mah-nah-gah-ray.
Axe,	Owen.
All,	Oyeant.
Arm,	Praw.
After a while,	Po-naie goie.
Antelope,	Quah-ratse.
Antelope skin,	Quah-ray empue.
A broom,	Shocoo-witse wene.
Americans,	Swap.
A tribe of Yutes,	Sampita.
Arrapahoes,	Shahray-tick-ah.
A file,	Te mah-tsone,
A pillow,	Tsopah-tagay.
A frying pan,	Taywah-yeang.
A tin pan,	Tooshah an-goots.
Awl,	Weyo.

conditions that the Cherokees welcomed the printer John Fisher Wheeler to the Union Mission Station on Grand River in present-day Oklahoma. There the American Board of Commissioners for Foreign Missions supplied him with a press, and in August 1835 he began printing primers, readers, and the like for the Creek Indians.

FOR ALMOST ALL American settlers, however, the Indian Territory was a region to be traveled through on the way to the new Promised Land of Oregon. In the mid-1830s a small trickle of settlers made it to Oregon, and that trickle gradually increased year by year until, in 1843, nine hundred emigrants made the journey, during what was known as the "Great Migration." In the next year that total was easily exceeded, as twelve hundred emigrants traveled along the Oregon Trail, and by 1845, the year Texas was annexed, the Oregon Territory boasted a population of more than six thousand U.S. settlers. Soon, largely in response to the discovery of gold in California, the population along the Pacific coast would explode, as tens of thousands of emigrants crossed the western plains, mountains, and deserts in search of a better life.

What role did books and reading play on the long overland trek? Books had always had a place on the frontier, but one that was too often taken for

granted, and so they have figured little in contemporary accounts. Nonetheless, from other evidence we know that books were an integral and essential part of most settler's household belongings and even sometimes a part of a frontiersman's kit. We know Daniel Boone carried a book or two with him during his treks through the wilderness of Kentucky, something Theodore Roosevelt remarked on:

Other hunters also came into the Kentucky wilderness, and Boone joined a small party of them for a short time. Such a party of hunters is always glad to have anything wherewith to break the irksome monotony of the long evenings passed round the camp fire; and a book or a greasy pack of cards was as welcome in a camp of Kentucky riflemen in 1770 as it is to a party of Rocky Mountain hunters in 1888. Boone has recorded in his own quaint phraseology an incident of his life during this summer, which shows how eagerly such a little band of frontiersmen read a book, and how real its characters became to their minds. He was encamped with five other men on Red River, and they had with them for their "amusement the history of Samuel Gulliver's travels, wherein he gave an account of his young master, Glumdelick, careing him on a market day for a show to a town called Lulbegrud." In the party who, amid such strange surroundings, read and listened to Dean Swift's writings was a young man named Alexander Neely. One night he came into camp with two Indian scalps, taken from a Shawnese village he had found on a creek running into the river; and he announced to the circle of grim wilderness veterans that "he had been that day to Lulbegrud, and had killed two Brobdignags in their capital." To this day the creek by which the two luckless Shawnees lost their lives is known as Lulbegrud Creek.

In the early 1830s Alexis de Tocqueville came upon a frontier settler's home and described what he found:

A single window with a muslin curtain; on a hearth of trodden clay an immense fire, which lights the whole interior; above the hearth, a good rifle, a deerskin, and plumes of eagles' feathers; on the right hand of the chimney, a map of the United States, raised and shaken by the wind through the crannies in the wall; near the

Scenes of Wonder and Curiosity in California was first published in San Francisco, in 1860, by Hutchings & Rosenfield. Its author, James M. Hutchings (1818–1902), was born in England and traveled to California in 1849, where he wrote about what he saw there, taking an artist with him to sketch illustrations as he made his way to Yosemite Valley.

"The Prairie Schooner," from James Mason Hutchings, *Scenes of Wonder and Curiosity in California* (San Francisco: A. Roman, 1871), 35. Susan B. Anthony Collection, Rare Book and Special Collections Division, Library of Congress.

map, on a shelf formed of a roughly hewn plank, a few volumes of books: a Bible, the first six books of Milton, and two of Shakespeare's plays; along the wall, trunks instead of closets; in the center of the room, a rude table, with legs of green wood with the bark still on them, looking as if they grew out of the ground on which they stood; but on this table a teapot of British china, silver spoons, cracked teacups, and some newspapers.

We might well wonder how typical this frontier cabin was with its Shakespeare and Milton. Almost certainly one would find a Bible and perhaps a newspaper, but more typical would be an almanac, some religious sermons or tracts, and possibly a popular novel by Scott or Cooper. For many readers, though, these popular novels were not considered proper and were looked down upon as a waste of time.

Books have always provided companionship during long periods of inactivity. When young William Cody, not yet known as Buffalo Bill, broke his leg in 1859 far from any settlement during a winter trapping trip in western Kansas, his companion had to leave him alone for almost a month while he went for help. "We had brought with us a number of books, and these I read through most of my waking hours." Though Cody may have grown tired of reading as each uneventful day passed, he must have soon wished that those days had never ended. After twelve days, he was discovered by a Sioux war party. "I made up my mind it was all over but the scalping." But luck was with Cody that day, as the chief, Rain-in-the-Face, was known to him. Cody had met him at Fort Laramie and had learned the Sioux language from his children. "I asked him if he intended to kill the boy who had been his children's playmate." After some consultation, the chief decided to spare Cody's life but to confiscate all his possessions, including his guns and all his provisions, leaving him with an old deer carcass and a fire. Perhaps they took the books as well, because Cody did not mention them again. He endured another seventeen days entombed under mounds of snow in his dugout with bands of wolves endeavoring to get in at him before the return of his companion. As Cody put it, "How I endured it I do not know. But the Plains teach men and boys fortitude."

John Forster, who wrote a celebrated biography of Charles Dickens, recounted a similar cohabitation with books which occurred at about the same time young Cody was laid up.

Twelve or thirteen years ago I crossed the Sierra Nevada mountains as a government surveyor under a famous frontiersman and civil engineer—Colonel Lander.

We were too early by a month, and became snow-bound just on the very summit. Under these circumstances it was necessary to abandon the wagons for a time, and drive the stock [mules] down the mountains to the valleys where there was a pasturage and running water. This was a long and difficult task, occupying several days. On the second day, in a spot where we expected to find nothing more human than a grizzly bear or an elk, we found a little hut, built of pine boughs and a few rough boards clumsily hewn out of small trees with an axe. The hut was covered with snow many feet deep, excepting only the hole in the roof which served for a chimney, and a small pit-like place in front to permit egress. The occupant came forth to hail us and solicit whisky and tobacco. He was dressed in a suit made entirely of flour-sacks, and was curiously labelled on various parts of his person *Best Family Flour. Extra.* His head was covered by a wolf's skin drawn from the brute's head—with the ears standing erect in a fierce alert manner. He was a most extraordinary object, and told us he had not seen a human being in four months. He lived on bear and elk meat and flour, laid in during his short summer. Emigrants in the season paid him a kind of ferry-toll. I asked him how he passed his time, and he went to a barrel and produced *Nicholas Nickleby* and *Pickwick*. I found he knew them almost by heart.

Books could make what otherwise might be a dreary and monotonous life bearable. This was particularly true for women. One Illinois woman described her passion for reading:

No man can run a farm without some one to help him, and in this case I have always been called upon and expected to help to do anything that a man would be expected to do; I began this when we were first married, when there were few household duties and no reasonable excuse for refusing to help.

I always had a passion for reading; during girlhood it was along educational lines; in young womanhood it was for love stories, which remained ungratified because my father thought it was sinful to read stories of any kind, and especially love stories. Later, when I was married, I borrowed everything I could find in the line of novels and stories and read them by stealth still, for my husband thought it was a willful waste of time to read anything and that it showed a lack of love for him if I would rather read than talk to him when I had a few moments of leisure, and, in order to avoid giving offense and still gratify my desire. I would only read when he was not at the house. . . .

In reading miscellaneously I got glimpses now and then of the great poets and authors, which aroused a great desire for a thorough perusal of them all; but up till the present time I have not been permitted to satisfy this desire. As the years have rolled on there has been more work and less leisure until it is only by the greatest effort that I may read current news.

Clearly for some, reading was not an easy activity. It had to be justified as moral and useful. Recreational reading was obviously neither of these, and a reader in such a situation had to take considerable risks. But, at least for this Illinois farm wife, those risks were worth it.

There can be little doubt that books were to be found in the baggage of the overland travelers. But the question remains as to which books. Certainly the Bible was the most prominent book, but what of the recreational kinds of books such as novels, romances, and tales of adventure? A great many diaries and letters written during the overland trek exist, but in them there are very few references to books. Perhaps this should not be surprising as books and reading were so much a part of the emigrants' culture that mention was unnecessary. The very fact that so many diaries were written on the trail is indicative of the place of the written or printed word in the lives of the pioneers. Writing a diary was not an easy thing to keep up along the trail, and in most cases it fell to women to write these accounts.

Eugenia Zieber noted that writing "must be done in snatches or at any moment, or not at all." Elizabeth Dixon Smith explained: "some times I would not get the chance to write for 2 or 3 days and then would have to rise in the night when my babe and all hands was a sleep light a candle and write." When her husband fell ill, she assumed responsibility for the journey. "The whole care of everything now falls upon my shoulders," she wrote in her diary before a silence of almost a week, "I cannot write any more at present." For one accustomed to a writing desk or even a table, a Conestoga wagon was most unsatisfactory. Phoebe Stanton noted: "My oportunyty for writing is poor as I have to write on a small box in the waggon with every kind of noise around me." She asks her reader to "forgive my scribling for I have written the most of it with the oxen hiched to the wagon." Just as the wagon provided little in the way of a satisfactory writing platform, it was equally unsatisfactory in protecting paper, writing implements, books, and people from the excesses of the weather. Jean Rio Baker, a Mormon widow who journeyed overland in 1851, wrote, "While I am now writing the claps of thunder are awful, they seem to be all round us at once, our vehicles shake violently at every clap." Anna Marie Morris reported an "awful wind storm" near the Arkansas River where she saw her "portfolios blowing open &

THE

PRAIRIE TRAVELER.

A HAND-BOOK FOR

OVERLAND EXPEDITIONS.

WITH MAPS, ILLUSTRATIONS, AND ITINERARIES OF
THE PRINCIPAL ROUTES BETWEEN THE
MISSISSIPPI AND THE PACIFIC.

BY RANDOLPH B. MARCY,
CAPTAIN U. S. ARMY.

PUBLISHED BY AUTHORITY OF THE WAR DEPARTMENT

NEW YORK:
HARPER & BROTHERS, PUBLISHERS,
FRANKLIN SQUARE.
1859.

One of the many overland guides available in the mid-nineteenth century was issued by the authority of the War Department in 1859. Randolph Marcy, author of *The Prairie Traveler*, was a captain in the army with extensive experience in the field. He described in great detail the army's approach to travel across the western expanses, and although his guide included much useful information for the overland emigrant, the book was not written for the typical family traveling westward on the overland trail.

Title page from Randolph Barnes Marcy, *The Prairie Traveler* (New York: Harper & Brothers, 1859). General Collections, Library of Congress.

scattering papers to the winds all over the Prairie." Writing was not an effortless task on the trail, but obviously it was a valued one.

We do catch a few glimpses of books, even those of a recreational nature, in these diaries. On the trail Lorena L. Hays noted that she read books "of conjugal affection" by such authors as "Lady Fanshawe and Mrs. Hutchinson." Reading was a regular activity for many children, who favored such titles as *The Life of Daniel Boone*, *Pilgrim's Progress*, and *Robinson Crusoe*. We also know books were carried along the trail because they were sometimes abandoned there. Albert Jerome Dickson noted that "books, furniture, knickknacks, china, daguerreotypes, guitars ... were the first things to be discarded" when the going got rough. Sterling Clark, an unmarried man on the trail, reported that he gave his books to Captain McLane and Major Rough at Fort Kearney, because he feared they would be ruined by being exposed to the elements during the journey.

Those without books, or new books, yearned for them. Lucena Parsons lamented this lack as her company waited for the snow to melt in the Sierras: "This is a warm sultry morning & I hardly know how to spend the day. There is no place of worship to go to & no new thing to read, so I spend part of the day in bed & the rest in thinking of home." One good indication of how many books were brought along is found in the words of a frontier teacher, India Harris Simmons, who called on the families of her students to create a school library from the books they possessed.

An illustration from Marcy's *The Prairie Traveler* shows varieties of camp chairs that can be constructed for use on the trail.

"Camp Chairs," from Randolph Barnes Marcy, *The Prairie Traveler* (New York: Harper & Brothers, 1859), plate k. General Collections, Library of Congress.

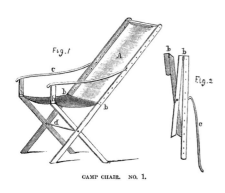

CAMP CHAIR. NO. 1.

CAMP CHAIRS. NOS. 2 AND 3.

K

The nondescript supply of books which each pupil had brought from whatever state was "back home" to him was placed on the bench by his side. Slates, which had to take the place of both blackboard and tablets, were of all sizes and descriptions, from Jimmy's tiny one with the red felt covered frame and pencil tied to it with a string, to Mary's big double one with the wide home-made frames fastened together with strong hinges and cut deep with initials and hearts. She had found it packed away among grandfather's books, which he had used away back in Ohio. There were histories from Illinois, spellers and writing books from Iowa, readers from St. Louis city schools, and even some old blue-backed spellers, with their five-syllabled puzzlers.

The guidebook was the most common secular book on the trail. Some guidebooks provided detailed information about the trail, and others gave more general advice on how to pack a wagon, what to take, and how to survive. One of these more general guides was written by Randolph Marcy, a captain in the U.S. Army, who offered the following advice in *The Prairie Traveler: A Handbook for Overland Expeditions* in 1859:

Bacon should be packed in strong sacks of a hundred pounds to each; or in very hot climates, put in boxes and surrounded with bran, which in a great measure prevents the fat from melting away.

Flour should be packed in stout double canvas sacks well sewed, a hundred pounds in each sack.

Butter may be preserved by boiling it thoroughly, and skimming off the scum as it rises to the top until it is quite clear like oil. It is then placed in tin canisters and soldered up. This mode of preserving butter has been adopted in the hot climate of southern Texas, and it is found to keep sweet for a great length of time, and its flavor is but little impaired by the process.

Sugar may be well secured in India-rubber or gutta-percha sacks, or so placed in the wagon as not to risk getting wet. Desiccated or dried vegetables are almost equal to the fresh, and are put up in such a compact and portable form as easily to be transported over the plains. They have been extensively used in the Crimean war and by our own army in Utah, and have been very generally approved. They are prepared by cutting the fresh vegetables into thin slices and subjecting them to a very powerful press, which removes the juice and leaves a solid cake, which after having been thoroughly dried in an oven, becomes almost as hard as a rock. A small piece of this, about half the size of a man's hand, when boiled, swells up so as to fill a vegetable dish, and is sufficient for four men. It is believed that the antiscorbutic properties of vegetables are not impaired by desiccation, and they will keep for years if not exposed to dampness. Canned vegetables, are very good for campaigning, but are not so portable as when put up in the other form.

Not all emigrants had the benefit of guidebooks and, as James Bennett commented in 1850, some "had neglected to inform themselves with regard to the route [and] had started on the desert without water" with potentially fatal results.

Guidebooks such as Joel Palmer's *Journal of Travels over the Rocky Mountains* (1847) provided detailed, mile-by-mile, information on the route west. Many emigrants followed these guidebooks with great devo-

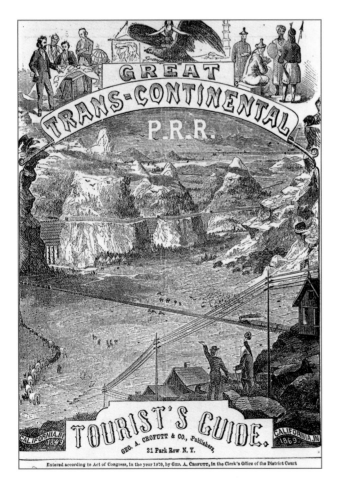

On May 10, 1869, when the tracks of the Union Pacific joined those of the Central Pacific at Promontory, Utah, the transcontinental railroad became a reality, and with it came a new kind of overland guidebook. Beginning in 1869, George Crofutt issued an annual guidebook for rail travelers that continued to appear over the next twenty-five years. The guidebook was initially entitled the *Great Trans-Continental Tourist's Guide from the Atlantic to the Pacific Ocean*, in 1878 became *Crofutt's New Overland Tourist and Pacific Coast Guide*, and in 1888 finally became *Crofutt's Overland Tours*. Consisting of about 250 pages, several folding maps, and many illustrations, Crofutt's guide was something no tourist could afford to be without.

Title page from George A. Crofutt, *Great Trans-Continental Tourists' Guide* (New York: Geo. A. Crofutt & Co., Publishers, 1870). General Collections, Library of Congress.

tion. When Eliza Ann McAuley noted in her diary in 1852 that her party had deviated from the prescribed path, she was obviously concerned: "As our guide book crosses to the south side of the [Platte] River at Fort Laramie, and we keep to the north side, we are following the trail without knowing what is ahead of us." Although there was overall agreement on the general route, each guidebook attempted to demonstrate its superiority over competitors, and each had its advocates among the emigrants. Disputes could arise when different guidebooks were consulted, as was the case which James Bennett noted "between Mr. Mills and Mr. Sweasy concerning the distance between our encampment and the forks of the Platte: each having gained information from different sources." A number of emigrant diaries show how closely the guidebooks were read. Not only were passages quoted from them, but errors were noted. James Bennett quoted from Palmer's guidebook describing Chimney Rock. When his party reached Soda Springs, he wrote "I shall not attempt a description of them, but refer the reader to Fremont and others who have visited this wonderful place." On the other hand, Eliza Ann McAuley wrote that areas her guidebook noted as barren proved to be fruitful. In 1850 Anna Marie Morris, who together with her husband was traveling in a military wagon train, was counting miles carefully along the Santa Fe trail, and she dutifully corrected her guidebook when she found it in error. Some were not at all satisfied with the guidebooks available. In 1851 Elizabeth Wood wrote about "Mr. Noosam, who is keeping a journal, with the intention of having it published for the benefit of the future emigration. It is the best guide I have seen, shows the road much better than Palmer's, gives more in detail the particulars, and its statements are to be relied upon."

Books had the power to sustain the pioneers on the trail. The Bible provided spiritual nourishment and was a guidebook for living. The guidebooks laid out the physical route for the emigrants and imparted secular wisdom. It could be argued that these two books provided all that was required to traverse the dangers of the Great American Desert and the Rocky Mountains and so to arrive safely in Oregon or California. But, as we have seen, other kinds of books also provided sustenance and intellectual nourishment. Popular novels and tales of adventure, although less visible in the overland accounts, were no doubt carried along the trail and passed from reader to reader. All kinds of books and reading material were carried westward, and were all the more valued as the vessels of American culture in the vastness of the West.

This illustration of Sutter's Mill, where gold was first discovered in 1848, appeared in the second edition of Laura Preston's *A Popular History of California,* which was published by Anton Roman in San Francisco in 1883. At the end of the book appears the following notice: "Agents Wanted in every town and county on this coast to sell Valuable Standard Subscription Books. For terms and territory, address A. Roman, 120 Sutter Street, San Francisco, Cal. New and Important subscription books just coming to hand. Old and experienced canvassers, please give this notice your special attention. Persons desiring to enter the canvas as beginners will never have a better opportunity."

"Sutter's Mill, 1851," frontispiece from Laura Preston, *A Popular History of California* (San Francisco: A. Roman, 1883).

CHAPTER FOUR

THE LAST FRONTIER

The American claim is by the right of manifest destiny
to overspread and possess the whole continent which Providence
has given us for the development of the great experiment of liberty
and federative self-government entrusted to us. . . . It is in our future
far more than in our past . . . that our True Title is found.

—John O'Sullivan, *New York Morning News*, 1845

From the first Spanish explorations along the California coast and the establishment of the missions in the eighteenth century, books and reading had played a natural role in society, but printing came to California only in 1834. In that year Agustin Juan Vicente Zamorano, secretary to the governor, imported an American-made press that came from Boston by way of Hawaii and established it in Monterey. He employed two printers and used the press to produce official pronouncements and similar items. The press was operated both in Monterey and Sonoma, always as an organ of the government, and never in any larger capacity.

At that time, Mexico had at best a very tenuous hold on California and was unable to resist the seizure of the territory in 1846, first by American settlers in the short-lived Bear Flag Revolt in June, and then by Commodore Robert F. Stockton, who raised the American flag on July 7. Officially, California was ceded to the United States as part of the settlement following the Mexican War in the Treaty of Guadalupe Hidalgo, signed February 2, 1848. The original Zamorano press was seized in Monterey by Walter Colton and Robert Semple, who, in traditional frontier form, then established a newspaper, the *Californian*, on August 15, 1846. The newspaper was printed by Medare Foisy, who had recently arrived from Oregon and the Lapwai mission in present-day Idaho.

(21)

co, y que así mismo se prohibira
á los buques ecstrangeros el comer-
cio de escala y cabotaje.

Hé dicho y por conclusion repito,
que si el Gobierno no toma en con-
sideracion mis reflecciones por que así
lo estímare conveniente, ó por que los
fundamentos de donde parte no se
estimen suficientes para conseguir el
fin propuesto, no por eso deja de
ocuparme el placer de haber procu-
rado hacer un servicio á mi patri-
a, aun concitandome, sin justicia, la
odiosidad de los que empeñados ecs-
clusivamente en negociar su bien particular, viven desentendidos del bene-
ficio y causa comun.

Sonoma Agosto 17 de 1837.

Mariano G. Vallejo.

Agustín V. Zamorano (1798–1842), executive secretary of the Mexican territory of Alta California, introduced the first printing press to California in
1834. It had come all the way from Boston by way of Hawaii to Monterey.
Zamorano hired two printers to run the press, which they did until an
uprising in November 1836, after which the press moved to Sonoma. The
Ecspocision, illustrated here, was printed in Sonoma in August 1837. The
twenty-one-page pamphlet, addressed to the governor and advocating commercial reforms, was written by Mariano G. Vallejo, the highest ranking
military officer in California. Vallejo explained, "I wrote the attached statement of which I sent the original to the governor of the State and which I
printed immediately in the small printing office that I had in Sonoma and of
which I was the only employee; I had the printed copies distributed throughout all parts of California and furthermore I gave some copies to the captains
of merchant ships that were going to ports in the United States of America."

*Ecspocision [sic] que hace el comdanante [sic] general interino de la Alta Califor-
nia al gobernador de la misma* (Sonoma: Agustín V. Zamorano, after August 17,
1837). Rare Book and Special Collections Division, Library of Congress.

For most of the fourteen thousand people in California, half of them
being American settlers, life remained much as it had been. Yet only about
a week before California officially became U.S. territory, events were
occurring that would transform the lives of almost every Californian, and
indeed, of most Americans. On January 24, 1848, James Marshall, a
carpenter in the employ of John Sutter, had made a remarkable discovery.
Sutter had established what amounted to a small empire in the interior of
California and had sent Marshall and a group of workmen into the mountains to set up a sawmill on the South Fork of the American River in the
Coloma Valley. Here on January 24 he found a nugget of gold in the
streambed. Sutter swore all the men to silence, but his attempt to keep the
lid on such momentous news was futile. Within days a few men were
scraping gold out of nooks and crannies with knives and other simple
implements.

Into this scene strode Samuel Brannan, a sometime Mormon and
newly established shopkeeper, who immediately saw in the miners a new
clientele for his store. He immediately acquired a bottle full of gold dust,
took it to San Francisco, and on May 12 announced to anyone who would

listen, "Gold! Gold! Gold from the American River!" This announcement convinced many San Franciscans, and within weeks the city emptied out in a stampede for the mountains. A San Francisco newspaper reported: "The whole country . . . resounds with the sordid cry of 'gold! Gold! *Gold!*' while the field is left half planted, the house half built, and everything neglected but the manufacture of shovels and pick axes." Walter Colton, now the mayor of Monterey, noted: "All were off for the mines, some on horses, some on carts, and some on crutches, and one went in a litter."

Soon word of the strike spread to Oregon, Hawaii, Mexico, and Peru, and a steady stream of prospectors began to pass through San Francisco. Almost all of these men continued through the new tent city of Sacramento, where Sam Brannan was more than happy to sell the arriving gold-diggers all the necessary supplies. Prices skyrocketed: a barrel of flour that used to cost twenty dollars now could bring as much as eight hundred dollars and eggs cost as much as three dollars each. In nine weeks in the summer of 1848 Brannan made more than thirty-six thousand dollars.

It took a considerable time for word to reach the East, and when the first reports came in, they were met with disbelief. But as report followed report of the fabulous riches to be plucked up off the ground in California, disbelief began to turn into frenzied action. On December 5, 1848, President Polk sent word to Congress: "The accounts of the abundance of gold in that territory are of such an extraordinary character as would scarcely command belief were they not corroborated by the authentic reports of officers in the public service." Two days later Colonel Richard Mason arrived in Washington, D.C., carrying with him 230 ounces of pure California gold. There could be no denying the truth of the reports now.

As the new year of 1849 dawned, more than 100,000 people began to move west to California. Of these, 30,000 went overland, following much of the Oregon Trail before cutting off to California, and almost all of them started out from Independence, Missouri, in the spring of 1849. This river of humanity moving west dwarfed any of the wagon trains of previous years and must have astonished the Indians through whose country it moved. Alonzo Delano was a part of that river. He described the scene on May 21, 1849:

For miles, to the extent of vision, an animated mass of beings broke upon our view. Long trains of wagons with their white covers were moving slowly along, a multitude of horsemen were prancing on the road, companies of men were traveling on foot, and although the scene was not a gorgeous one, yet the display of banners from many wagons, and the multitude of armed men, looked as if a mighty army was on its march; and in a few moments we took our station in the line, a component part of the motley throng of gold seekers, who were leaving home and friends far behind, to encounter the peril of mountain and plain.

Among the fortune seekers was a young German, Anton Roman, who arrived in California in 1849. He immediately made his way to the gold fields on the Trinity River at Weaverville in the Shasta region of northern California. At Scott Bar he had some success and slowly amassed a sizable quantity of gold dust. In December 1851 he visited San Francisco. Anton found it a wild and vibrant city full of untutored wealth, eager to acquire the hallmarks of culture, particularly books. A contemporary visitor described the scene: "The bookstores of San Francisco drive a thriving trade after the arrival of each mail, but the importations consist for the most part of novels, which are greedily bought up, and find a ready sale in the mining regions." Some of these books never made it to the bookstores and were being sold by "A live Yankee [who] has adopted the plan of traveling up and down Long Wharf, with a horse and wagon, the latter filled with literature for sale, of every description, from the horrifying yellow covered stories of robberies and murderers up to the classics and histories." In 1851 the newspaper *Alta California* had reported: "The reading community of San Francisco are not obliged as formerly to spend their leisure hours in poring over the pages of some old book which has found its way around Cape Horn, or across the Isthmus of Panama. Now we receive by every steamer the latest publications . . . solid bound books, and the yellow covered whilers away of careless hours."

Anton Roman did not discover this Yankee salesman, but instead entered the bookstore of Burgess, Gilbert and Still. John Hamilton Still had established the first bookstore in San Francisco in 1849, and on January 7, 1850, he was advertising in the *Alta California*. On February 28 he wrote to his mother: "Since I last wrote to you I moved my store from Pike Street down in the square of Plaza, which is the most business part of the city. My store is ten feet by fourteen in size and I have to pay four hundred dollars per month for it besides $300 a month more for clerks, in the shape of three boys." Clearly the costs of doing business in

San Francisco were very high, but so also was the potential for profit. One bookseller recalled years later that he had sold a secondhand copy of *Webster's Dictionary*, which sold for five dollars new in the East, for twenty-five dollars in San Francisco. Such inflated prices were not a permanent feature of San Francisco bookselling, but while they lasted, the trade was highly unstable, partnerships were made and unmade, and fortunes and bankruptcies followed one upon another. John Hamilton Still persevered and attracted many customers, among them the young German miner.

Anton Roman had not been brought up in the book trade, but books, as they did for so many people, held a natural attraction for him. He cast his eyes over the rows of volumes offered by Burgess, Gilbert and Still and remembered the utter dearth of books in the mining camps and how the miners valued the few books available to them in the mountains. At that point, he resolved to spend his gold, over one hundred ounces, to purchase books that he would in turn sell to the literature-starved miners in Shasta. Like Samuel Brannan, he would mine gold from the miners rather than from the earth, which in point of fact was much more of a sure thing.

Roman peddled his books from camp to camp with great success. Life in the camps was unlike anything most of the men had ever experienced, but the camps were full of literate men who lacked reading material. Alonzo Delano described the miners and one of the camps:

The population ... represented almost every State in the Union, while France, England, Ireland, Germany and even Bohemia had their delegates. As soon as breakfast was dispatched, all hands were engaged in digging and washing gold in the banks, or in the bed of the stream. When evening came, large fires were built, around which the miners congregated, some engrossed with thoughts of home and friends, some to talk of new discoveries, and richer diggings somewhere else; or, sometimes a subject of debate was started, and the evening was whiled away in pleasant, and often instructive, discussion, while many, for whom this kind of recreation had not excitement enough, resorted to dealing monte, on a small scale, thus either exciting or keeping up a passion for play. Some weeks were passed in this way under the clear blue sky of the mountains, and many had made respectable piles. I highly enjoyed the wild scenery, and, quite as well, the wild life we were leading, for there were many accomplished and intelligent men; and a subject for amusement or debate was rarely wanting. As for ceremony or dress, it gave us no trouble: we were all alike.

Roman set up shop in Shasta City, where on March 12, 1853, there appeared an advertisement for the Shasta Book Store, which featured "a large and splendid assortment of Books and Stationery . . . at the lowest prices. Among the late works just received are the following: The Necromances, Parricide . . . Fair Rosamond, Amy Lawrence, Mad Cap . . . Stanley Thorn . . . &c. Also, the works of Shakespeare, Byron, Milton, Gray, Campbell and other distinguished poets. All the latest newspapers, both home and foreign, constantly on hand." In addition Roman sold musical instruments, having "just received an assortment of . . . Flutes, Flagolets, Clarionets," and songbooks. Literary taste in the camps tended toward the more popular titles, as Roman well knew, and he featured those works ahead of the traditional works of "distinguished poets." The bookseller apparently found many eager customers as by the autumn of 1853 he had spent over $42,000 on stock, which certainly returned a sizable profit.

Along with the whole region, the book trade had expanded dramatically during these years. In addition to booksellers, there were book

Anton Roman's Shasta Book Store was among the principal buildings of the new California town shown in this bird's-eye view of Shasta. His bookstore was part of the Callaghan Block depicted in the vignette at bottom center. Drawn by Charles C. Kuchel and Emil Dresel in San Francisco and then printed by Britton & Rey, this lithograph was published by Roman in 1856 and sold in Shasta. Such city views were very popular and were a source of great civic pride.

Shasta, 1856. Shasta County, California, 1856. Toned lithograph (hand colored), with 23 vignettes, by Charles Conrad Kuchel, published by A. Roman, 1856. Courtesy of the Amon Carter Museum, Fort Worth, Texas (1972.127).

binders and printers. One printer trumpeted his abilities in the *Illustrated California Almanac for 1855*:

We have recently made large additions to our job printing office and take pleasure in informing our friends, customers, and the public in general, that we are now better than ever before, prepared to execute all kinds of Plain and Ornamental printing. . . . For printing Books, Pamphlets, Catalogues, blanks or small posters, we have now in operation a New Patent Adams Power Press, the only one of its kind now in California, and which for the execution of Fine Work is not surpassed by any press now manufactured. For Printing Bill heads, circulars, etc., we use one of the Ruggles's Patent Machine Presses, capable of throwing off 1,500 impressions per hour. . . . For Printing Marriage, Address, Ball tag or business cards, we have one of R. Hoe & Co's Patent Card Presses which will print, with ease, 1,200 cards per hour. . . . For printing large mammoth posters, either in black or colored Inks, we have a large sized Washington Hand press, just received from the manufacture of R. Hoe & Co., New York; also a large assortment of Cuts, suitable for Posters, such as Steamers, River Boats, Clipper Ships, Railroad, etc., etc.

Various kinds of "public" or social libraries were created in California, as many of the settlers who had enjoyed such libraries in the East desired to recreate them in the West. S. P. Dewey, who had brought 320 volumes with him from the East, donated them in 1850 to help create the library of the Mercantile Library Association of Sacramento. Writing to the association, he said: "Having been myself for near twenty years the recipient of the benefits of a similar institution [the Mercantile Library of New York City], I am prepared to appreciate the great benefits this community must derive from your association." The Mercantile Library Association gladly accepted Dewey's generous gift and organized a subscription library, its members to pay five dollars to join and five dollars per quarter. Duly established, the library unfortunately was destroyed in the fire of November 1852 that razed most of Sacramento. A total loss, it was never reestablished. In 1854 the Pioneer Society began collecting books, and in 1855 the Order of Odd Fellows established a small library, but neither of these was open to the public.

The citizens of Sacramento tried again to create a public library in 1857, when they organized the Sacramento Library Association. Joseph W. Winans, a former member of the defunct Mercantile Library Association and a private book collector whose personal library exceeded five thousand volumes in 1878, was named chairman, but perhaps the association's most notable members were Collis P. Huntington, Mark Hopkins, Leland Stanford, and Charles Crocker, the "Big Four" who would earn vast fortunes in building the Central Pacific railroad. With such substantial support, the association was capitalized at $25,000, but its annual revenues never exceeded its expenses. The Sacramento Library Association continued to operate at a loss until the city took it over in 1879. Regardless of financial solvency, however, it provided the citizens of Sacramento with ready access to books.

In 1857 Anton Roman acquired a large stock of books from the East and set up a shop in San Francisco, still maintaining his extensive trade through the towns and mining camps in the interior. Roman was not alone in his desire to establish a bookstore. San Francisco at this time had an unusual concentration of bookstores, some containing as many as 100,000 volumes. In 1860 the federal census would rank California fifth in the nation in the number of bookstores. Obviously flourishing, by 1859 Roman was able to move into larger quarters at 158 Montgomery Street,

Sacramento was the jumping off point for the mines in the mountains. This 1850 lithograph, produced in New York, captures the great activity along the riverfront and pictures the Sierra Nevada in the distance.

Sacramento City, Ca., from the Foot of J Street, drawn by George V. Cooper; lithographed by William Endicott & Co.; published, New York: Stringer & Townsend, 1850. Prints and Photographs Division, Library of Congress (LC-USZ62-93402).

By 1851, the small village of San Francisco had been transformed into a bustling cosmopolitan center. In this lithograph by S. F. Marryat, which was printed by M. & N. Hanhart and published by Henry Squire & Co., the activity and diversity of the city are plainly evident in the figures in the foreground and the number of ships anchored in the harbor.

San Francisco, chromolithograph, drawn by S. F. Marryat; published, London: M. & N. Hanhart Chromo Lith., ca. 1851. Prints and Photographs Division, Library of Congress (LC-USZ62-7724).

described as "the largest and most elegant single room occupied for such purposes in San Francisco."

Like many booksellers before him, Roman soon began to think of publishing his own books. Though linked by sea and overland routes to the East, California remained an isolated market for local publishers. Books, new, as well as used, were imported in large numbers from the East, but the shipping costs wiped out the price advantage that the eastern firms used to undercut local publishers, and until the advent of the transcontinental railroad in 1869, California publishers were able to hold their own against such firms as Harper & Brothers in New York. Roman, though, had no intention of challenging the great eastern publishing houses and instead followed the long-established frontier custom of publishing works of local interest.

One of Roman's first books was printed at the *Alta California* job office in 1860. This slim volume, a talk given by Edmund Randolph before the Society of California Pioneers, was entitled *An Outline of the History of California, from the Discovery of the Country to the Year 1849*. Roman published four titles in 1860, but then nothing more until 1863. All three titles that he issued in 1863 were of a practical nature. One was John S. Hittell's *Resources of California, Comprising Agriculture, Mining, Geography, Climate, Commerce, ... and the Past and Future Development of the State* (1863), which was so successful that it went through several editions. Continuing in this line of California history, geography, and natural resources were such works as Laura Preston's *Youth's History of California* (1867), John Ferris's *Financial Economy of the United States Illustrated, and Some of the Causes Which Retard the Progress of California Demonstrated*

(1867), *A Sketch of the Route to California, China, and Japan, via the Isthmus of Panama* (1867), which promoted the Pacific Mail Steamship Company, and J. D. B. Stillman's *Seeking the Golden Fleece: A Record of Pioneer Life in California* (1876). Roman also published John Carey Cremony's *Life among the Apaches* (1868), which was dedicated to the publisher: "To the pioneer and liberal publisher, Anton Roman, the zealous and enterprising friend of literature on the Pacific Coast."

Roman recognized the growing need for Californians to understand the Orient. Thousands of Chinese were pouring into California to work on the railroads, trade with Asia was booming, and it was recognized that far too little was known about these new immigrants and the countries from which they came. Roman set out to remedy that. He established an Orientalia section in his book store and began in 1867 to publish such titles as A. W. Loomis's *Confucius and the Chinese Classics* (1867), in which Roman wrote: "No question is more frequently asked by curious and thinking people than this: What is the literature of the Chinese? They are a reading people; then what do they read? They are a peculiar people; what has made them so? They are an unchanging people; what is it that

At the height of his success, Anton Roman (1828–1903) looked every inch the prosperous publisher. The financial panic of 1873, however, prompted a series of reverses from which Roman would never recover. He died in a train accident at age seventy-five.

Anton Roman, photograph reproduced in Noah Brooks, "Early Days of the Overland," *Overland Monthly* 32 (July–December 1898): 6. Courtesy of Harvard College Library.

A. ROMAN & CO.'S PUBLICATIONS.

NEW AND ATTRACTIVE

CALIFORNIA JUVENILE BOOKS.

Elegantly Illustrated from Original Designs.

THE GOLDEN GATE SERIES.

By MAY WENTWORTH.

Three Volumes, Square 16mo, Extra Cloth, in a Neat Case, Price, $3.75.

COMPRISING

Fairy Tales from Gold Land.—First Series.
Fairy Tales from Gold Land.—Second Series.
Golden Dawn, and other Stories.

Any Volume sold separately. Price, $1.25.

THE INGLENOOK SERIES.

4 volumes, square 16mo. Extra cloth, in a neat case. Price, $5.00.

Inglenook. By CARRIE CARLTON.
The Candy Elephant, and other Stories. By CLARA G. DOLLIVER.
No Baby in the House, and other Stories. By CLARA G. DOLLIVER.
A Boy's Trip across the Plains. By LAURA PRESTON.

Any volume sold separately. Price, $1.25.

PHEBE TRAVERS:

Or, One Year at a French Boarding-School.

By AUNT FLORIDA.

18mo. Extra cloth. Price, 75 cents.

The Stories contained in these Juveniles are chiefly about California and the Pacific Coast; being interesting and instructive for Parents and Children. Californians will recognize many familiar places and personages

A. ROMAN & CO.,

PUBLISHERS AND BOOKSELLERS,

417 & 419 Montgomery St., San Francisco.
27 Howard St., New York.

*** *Copies sent by mail, post-paid, on receipt of price.*

Roman, like most publishers, placed advertisements at the back of his books. Here, at the end of *Scenes of Wonder and Curiosity in California*, he promoted his children's titles, emphasizing their California subjects.

Advertisement pages from James Mason Hutchings, *Scenes of Wonder and Curiosity in California* (San Francisco: A. Roman, 1871), following p. 292. Rare Book and Special Collections Division, Library of Congress.

has fixed their habits?" He also published Benoni Lanctot's *Chinese and English Phrase Book: With the Chinese Pronunciation Indicated in English, Specially Adapted for the Use of Merchants, Travelers, and Families* (1867), which was designed "to enable all classes of citizens, especially merchants, shipmasters, contractors, families, and travelers to acquire an elementary and practical knowledge of the spoken language of the Canton dialect . . . the most generally understood by all classes of Chinese immigrants on the Pacific Coast." For anyone desiring information on the Orient, Roman's bookstore on Montgomery Street was an essential stop.

Roman never forgot his time in the goldfields, and the books he published reflected the miner's need for practical books on technical subjects. These included Gregory Yale's *Legal Titles to Mining Claims and Water Rights in California* (1867) and William Barstow's *Sulphurets: What They Are, How Concentrated, How Assayed, and How Worked: With a Chapter on the Blowpipe Assay of Minerals* (1867). He stocked his bookstore with many other similar titles, such as Guido Küstel's *Nevada and California Processes of Silver and Gold Extraction* (published in San Francisco by F. D. Carlton in 1863 and reprinted in 1868).

Another kind of reading matter that was highly prized by the miners was of a more recreational nature, and Roman always turned a good profit in selling sensational novels and tales of adventure. He published a few such popular novels but began to look to the more refined kinds of literature. He chose to publish James Linen's *Poetical and Prose Writings* (1865 and 1866), A. W. Patterson's *Onward: A Lay of the West* (1869), Daniel Thomas Callaghan's *Madrona, etc.* (1876), and Charles Warren Stoddard's *Poems* (1867). This last volume was published by subscription in an elegant illustrated edition that was to be found in all the best homes in San Francisco.

In about 1862, San Franciscan Mary Tingley brought Roman a folder full of clippings of local poetry that she had collected from California newspapers over several years. Roman set the folder aside, letting it sit for a couple of years. And then, having met a former miner, now a journalist, with literary aspirations, he asked him to take the clippings and

Bret Harte (1836–1902) arrived in California in 1854, and after a stint in the mines settled in San Francisco in 1860 to work as a printer and then a journalist. For Anton Roman he edited a collection of local poetry entitled *Outcroppings* in 1865. In 1867 Harte produced a volume of his own verse, *The Lost Galleon,* and *Condensed Novels and Other Papers.* With such stories as "The Luck of Roaring Camp," he achieved national fame, which was, however, short-lived, and then spent his remaining years first in the East and then in England writing stories, novels, and plays that were pale imitations of his early California work.

Bret Harte, frontispiece portrait from *The Poetical Works of Bret Harte* (Boston and New York: Houghton, Mifflin and Co., 1883). General Collections, Library of Congress.

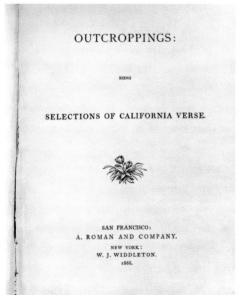

When *Outcroppings* appeared in 1865, a near riot occurred as every local poet descended on Roman's book shop to examine this first collection of California verse. Many poets discovered their poems had not been included and those poets who had been included disagreed with Harte's selection and treatment. Almost all agreed the title was inappropriate for such a volume. Harte's reaction to the controversy was that it "ought to make the volume sell."

Title page from Bret Harte, editor, *Outcroppings: Being Selections of California Verse* (San Francisco: A. Roman and Co., 1865; New York: W. J. Widdleton, 1866). Rare Book and Special Collections Division, Library of Congress.

create a book out of them. This young editor was Bret Harte, who was more than pleased to be given such an opportunity. Harte scoured the previous decade's newspapers for the works of local poets and combined his finds with Miss Tingley's clippings to create the volume *Outcroppings: Being Selections of California Verse*, which appeared in December 1865. Though Mary Tingley was given credit for her folder of clippings in Harte's preface, she apparently had no larger part in the book and received nothing in way of compensation. Outraged, she denounced Harte and Roman.

Controversy around the book did not end there. *Outcroppings* was the first published volume of California poetry, a handsome production on tinted paper and beautifully bound, and its inclusion (or exclusion) of a particular poet could make a reputation (or break it). Within hours of the book's publication a horde of poets and their devoted followers descended on Roman's book shop. Some were gratified, but most were dissatisfied with Harte's selections. All agreed that the title was inappropriate for a book of serious verse. The newspapers overflowed with outrage at the book: "As a collection of California poetry, it is beneath contempt." But Harte was not worried about the uproar and was overheard to remark, "All of which ought to make the volume sell." And indeed it did.

Roman's major competitor, Hubert Howe Bancroft, immediately asked Mary Wentworth Newman (who appeared as May Wentworth in print) to bring out a much larger collection of California poetry, *Poetry of the Pacific*, which was produced by the Pacific Publishing Company in 1867. Much more inclusive and graced with what everyone considered a suitable title, this volume was received with greater general approval by the San Francisco literati.

Bancroft had arrived in San Francisco in 1852, as a young twenty-year-old, only a few months after Roman had purchased his first lot of books. Born in Ohio, he had acquired some bookselling experience in Buffalo, New York, and he intended to follow that trade in California. In 1856, together with his brother Albert Bancroft, he opened a bookstore there. Hubert Howe Bancroft continued from success to success. By 1870 he had emerged as the city's foremost publisher and bookseller, and indeed was the largest and most noted bookseller west of Chicago. His business included printing, engraving, lithography, bookbinding, and even, like Roman, marketing sheet music and musical instruments.

Anton Roman remained Bancroft's major competition. Most of the books in Roman's shop in Montgomery Street—as was true of every other bookseller as well—were not his own publications, or even West Coast publications, but the products of the large publishing houses of New York, Boston, Philadelphia, and Chicago. Having originally specialized in books for miners, and books of local interest, Roman aimed to create a comprehensive bookstore. In 1861 he had issued his first catalog, 259 pages long, which included "a classified collection of prominent standard authors—

embracing a wide range . . . and of use to all seeking the best works in any branch of literature." He advertised that his shop had "the finest library bound books, embracing all the standard works in the English language . . . a complete stock in every department of literature." Here readers could find "the rarest and most costly editions of the poets and favorite authors of the age, together with the choicest gift-books and other *recherché* publications of the English and American press."

In 1865, only eight years after first setting up in the city, Roman was second only to Bancroft as the leading bookseller in San Francisco. He had annual sales of nearly $200,000 and his stock was valued at about $80,000. His stock consisted of 50,000 volumes of standard and miscellaneous books, 8,000 theological titles, 5,000 scientific books, 3,000 medical titles, and 500 military books. His success was built on the axiom of "quick sales and small profits." He noted that his "extensive and elegant assortment" of titles could be purchased "cheap for cash." Roman offered libraries special rates and advertised that particular care was exercised "in filling all wholesale and retail orders by mail and express, with promptness and at the lowest cash rate."

Roman had agents in New York, London, and Paris, but in 1866 he decided he needed a permanent presence in New York. He established a home in the city, which he maintained for six years, and solidified relations with the New York firm of William J. Widdleton, which had been acting as Roman's agent for some years. Roman arranged for his own publications to be copublished by Widdleton, and many of his books bear the double imprint of Roman in San Francisco and Widdleton in New York. This gave the San Franciscan an important edge in doing business in the East, both in terms of marketing his own publications and in acquiring stock for his bookshop. Books were typically shipped by sea and a considerable time could pass between the selection of a title in New York and its unpacking and placement on the shelf in San Francisco. While the books themselves were still on a slow boat, word of new books and authors reached readers in the West long before Roman could make these works available. It was greatly to Roman's advantage to have an establishment in New York that could anticipate the market in California and ship the books at the earliest moment possible. Roman noted, "We are constantly in receipt of all new publications by steamer as fast as issued from the press. Books imported to order on shortest notice."

With such interest in literature evident in the city, and in an attempt to

The first issue of the *Overland Monthly* appeared in July 1868. Modeling it on the *Atlantic,* publisher Anton Roman and his editor Bret Harte intended that "the nature and character of the magazine will embrace, to the fullest extent, the commercial and social interests of California and the Pacific Coast.... Our intentions are to have every article original [and] to employ only the best talent in the country." Harte explained that "The bear who adorns the cover may be 'an ill-favored' beast 'whom women cannot abide,' but he is honest withal. Take him if you please as the symbol of local primitive barbarism. He is crossing the track of the Pacific Railroad, and has paused a moment to look at the coming engine of civilization and progress." The magazine was a great success, and with only a single interruption from 1875 to 1880, it continued publication until 1935.

Title page, the *Overland Monthly* 1 (1868); San Francisco, A. Roman & Co. Rare Book and Special Collections Division, Library of Congress.

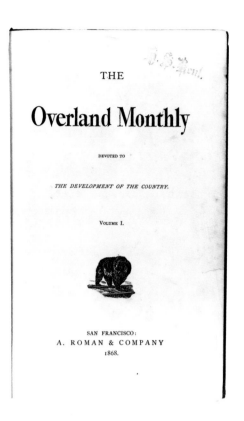

THE

Overland Monthly

DEVOTED TO

THE DEVELOPMENT OF THE COUNTRY.

VOLUME I.

SAN FRANCISCO:
A. ROMAN & COMPANY
1868.

get a jump on Bancroft, Roman decided the time was ripe to embark on a new venture, the launching of a literary magazine. Such enterprises were not uncommon in frontier cities when they reached a certain size, as we may recall from Cincinnati in the 1820s. But they were not without risk, as almost every literary magazine editor, including Cincinnatian Timothy Flint, had learned. Not to be deterred by the difficulties of his predecessors, Roman once again turned to Bret Harte to edit the magazine, which they decided to call the *Overland Monthly*. Roman issued an advertisement that illustrates his vision for the publication.

A. Roman & Co. propose taking immediate steps for issuing a first-class monthly magazine, the first number to appear July 1st, 1868. The nature and character of the magazine will embrace, to the fullest extent, the commercial and social interests of California and the Pacific Coast. ... Our intentions are to have every article original; to employ only the best talent in the country; to pay for every article; and to distribute 3000 copies monthly, until its permanent circulation reaches or exceeds this number. The rates of advertising will be $50 per page monthly, or $25 for a half page.

His appeal for advertising succeeded in bringing in about nine hundred dollars a month, and with this secure financial base the magazine was launched on schedule, at four dollars a year to subscribers.

In the inaugural issue, July 1868, Harte explained that the title, the *Overland Monthly*, represented "the highway of our thought . . . [and] what could be more appropriate for the title of a literary magazine than to call it after this broad highway?" Harte also contributed a new poem, "San Francisco"; Noah Brooks and W. C. Bartlett supplied a piece, "The Diamond Makers of Sacramento"; and B. P. Avery wrote on "Art Beginnings on the Pacific." The feature "Current Literature" surveyed new books, including, of course, those published by Roman.

Bret Harte had agreed to contribute new stories to the magazine, and Roman encouraged him to write about life in the mining camps. Harte's first such story, scheduled for the second number, was "The Luck of Roaring Camp." It was set in type and galley proofs were produced, but soon Roman's office was in an uproar. His proofreader, Mrs. Sarah B. Cooper, was outraged at what she termed the immorality of the story. Nonetheless, Roman ordered it published. "The Luck of the Roaring Camp" was a terrific success that brought Harte's name to wider attention and ensured the success of the magazine.

By October, Roman was ecstatic, and Harte proclaimed in that month's issue, "The prophet has been honored in his own country. Throughout the Pacific Slope, from San Diego to Portland; on the Sierras and along the Great Highway . . . wherever a printing press has been carried or a ream of paper packed, *The Overland* has been kindly welcomed." But Roman's part in the successful magazine was short-lived. He was ill, and his doctor recommended he leave the damp and cold climate of San Francisco. So, by the end of the year, Roman had sold the *Overland Monthly* to John H. Carmany for $7,500 and departed for a rest. The *Overland* was one of only a very few literary journals that found enduring success. With only a single interruption (1875–80), the magazine continued into the 1930s.

Roman's bookselling and publishing business was so good that in 1871 he moved to a new address on Montgomery Street. These "new and larger premises" at 11 Montgomery Street were lavishly appointed in walnut, the ceiling painted in fresco, all creating "a magnificent temple of letters." The "noble hall has its long tables covered with the choicest mental food culled from all climes and served up in the most magnificent style of binding." As Roman emphasized, "Here we are, geographically isolated from the world's throng, and yet the greatest cities cannot show a more complete establishment than ours." Indeed San Francisco could boast of all the amenities of any of the world's great cities, and though it still supplied many frontier communities in the hinterlands with goods, the immediate frontier had long receded.

Roman's triumph was short-lived. He was caught in the financial panic of 1873, which finally resulted in his bankruptcy in April 1879. Though he lost everything, he was not without plans for the future. In 1880 he established a new literary magazine, the *Californian*. The *Overland Monthly* had suspended publication in 1875, and Roman intended his new magazine to carry on the traditions of his former publication. He was so successful in this regard that the *Californian* would be transformed into the resurrected *Overland Monthly* (second series) in 1883. Again in 1881, however, this time because of his own financial difficulties, he was forced to sell his share of the magazine. In 1882, Roman tried to reenter the book trade, placing an advertisement in the *Californian*, announcing that "Mr. Roman has again started in Business as bookseller and publisher . . . and . . . is prepared to supply anything and everything in his line, from a sheet of note-paper to a complete library in bindings warranted to match the carpet. We mention this last with the special purpose of influencing the patronage of our rich men in his favor." Roman struggled on for a few years, mostly acting as an agent for subscription publishers, but by 1888 he had given up. He died in a train wreck in 1903.

Bancroft, on the other hand, had managed to avoid the disasters that overcame Roman. His business prospered, and whereas Roman's name has been all but forgotten, Bancoft's has found a permanent place in history, not only of California but also of the United States. This immortality was not a result of his business acumen or even his literary taste. Bancroft differed from Roman and his other fellow publishers and booksellers in his avid book collecting.

Beginning in about 1863, Bancroft began to collect books, pamphlets,

Hubert Howe Bancroft (1832–1918) was the most successful bookseller and publisher in late-nineteenth-century California. Not only did he create a prosperous publishing firm, but he was also a respected historian who published numerous histories related to the West. Finally, he collected one of the finest libraries devoted to the subject of the West, a library that bears his name today at the University of California, Berkeley.

Hubert Howe Bancroft, frontispiece portrait from Bancroft, *Literary Industries: A Memoir* (New York: Harper & Brothers, 1891). General Collections, Library of Congress.

and ephemeral materials, originally to compile a California guidebook. Many of these volumes came from the stock in his own bookstore. But his library soon became much more than a collection to support the production of a guidebook. It included "everything that bore on western history, whether it was prose or poetry, book or pamphlet, broadside or newspaper, authoritative or partisan. . . . It was my custom when collecting to glance through any book which I thought might contain information on the territory marked out. I made it no part of my duty at this time to enquire into the nature or quality of the production; . . . in making such a collection it is impossible to determine at a glance what is of value and what is not. The most worthless trash may prove some fact wherein the best book is deficient, and this makes the trash valuable." By 1870 his library consisted of more than sixty thousand volumes.

It was Bancroft's intention that the library should be used to write a definitive history of the Pacific Coast. He searched for historians and scholars to undertake the history, but when he found none, he undertook the task himself, aided by a staff of researchers and writers. One of the results was his thirty-nine-volume *History of the Pacific States* completed in 1890. The *History* was hailed as a historical landmark, but it was Bancroft's library that made a permanent contribution to the history and culture, not only of California but of the nation. Bancroft was collecting the history of a young region, and most of those who had shaped the history of the Pacific Coast were still alive. He was indefatigable in pursuing original documents from the estates of such important early figures as General Mariano Guadalupe Vallejo, the greatest landowner in old California, and Sir James Douglas, former governor of British Columbia. He had transcriptions made of documents he could not purchase, and when no documents existed, he interviewed important figures, creating what came to be known as "Bancroft Dictations," an early form of oral history.

Bancroft built a separate building to house his library, which, because of its construction of brick and its location out of the city center, survived the earthquake and fire of 1906 undamaged. San Francisco's other great library, Albert Sutro's extraordinary collection of more than 200,000 volumes, was completely consumed in the disaster. In 1905 Bancroft arranged to sell the library for a fraction of its worth to the University of California, where today the Bancroft Library is one of the world's great research libraries.

CHAPTER FIVE

THE FRONTIER IN BOOKS

There, for a time at least, we were Americans. We had our frontier.
We shall do ill indeed if we forget and abandon its strong lessons,
its great hopes, its splendid human dreams.

—Emerson Hough, *The Passing of the Frontier*, 1918

UNIQUE AMONG those of contemporary Western nations, the American national identity has been created from present and living memory. Unlike the modern English national identity, it was not created out of distant memories from an era many centuries past. The English visions, which hearkened back to Anglo-Saxon England and the mythical Arthurian realms, were mediated by small groups of scholars who alone could understand the ancient languages. The books those scholars wrote were then read by a narrow circle of educated people who reinterpreted the ancient histories and myths for the general public, and in time the sense of what medieval England had been and how it related to the present began to work its way into the popular conception of English history. By the eighteenth century the average Englishman was fully conscious of the Anglo-Saxon heritage that distinguished him from all other peoples and endowed him with an innate strength of character and democratic spirit. These modern Anglo-Saxons looked to the past with pride and to the future with a certainty in their own moral superiority and thus the righteousness of British imperial dominion. In America, it was the frontier experience that defined the nation's identity, and there was no need for scholarly mediation or a hearkening to the distant past. The general reader could read about the frontier even as he or she experienced it firsthand.

The first attempt to make sense of the new land was made by the Puritans, who for the most part rejected the wilderness and its inhabitants. William Bradford, in *Of Plymouth Plantation*, explained the Puritans' view: "The place they had thoughts on was some of those vast and unpeopled countries of America, which are fruitful and fit for habitation, being devoid of all civil inhabitants, where there are only savage and brutish men which range up and down, little otherwise than the wild beasts of the same." The Indians were both inconsequential and terrifying. On the one hand they were seen as uncivilized and thus no better than wild beasts, and therefore easily disregarded. On the other hand, the Indians appeared to be calculating men, capable of acts far more diabolical than any wild beasts might perpetrate. Thus they were perceived as devils, and the untamed wilderness that they inhabited was viewed as a dark and suspicious place. Bradford believed the settlers were

in continual danger of the savage people, who are cruel, barbarous, and most treacherous, being most furious in their rage and merciless where they overcome; not being content only to take away life, but delight to torment men in the most bloody manner that may be; flaying some alive with the shells of fishes, cutting off the members and joints of others by piecemeal and broiling on the coals, eat the collops of their flesh in their sight whilst they live, with other cruelties horrible to be related.

This view of the frontier was widely shared and crystallized in what came to be known as captivity narratives, tales of capture by the Indians. The first of these narratives to be printed was Mary Rowlandson's *Sovereignty and Goodness of God*, published in Cambridge, Massachusetts, in 1682. During King Philip's War, the Indians had attacked many towns and settlements across New England, including Lancaster, Massachusetts, where Rowlandson and her family lived. Many fatalities and casualties occurred on both sides, and Mary Rowlandson saw her neighbors and immediate members of her family killed before her eyes as the Indians overran Lancaster. Together with her three children, she was captured and carried off, and she suffered greatly as her two oldest children were taken away from her and her youngest child died. The narrative of *Sovereignty* describes her experiences. Bereft of "civilized" companionship and alone in the wilderness world, she found her sole comfort in her Bible.

From the Puritan perspective, Mary Rowlandson was in Hell, surrounded by devils. She was tempted to succumb to the pleasures of easy

The first captivity narrative to appear in print was Mary Rowlandson's *Sovereignty and Goodness of God* (1682). These accounts of capture by Indians emphasized God's will in times of great adversity and how the contemplation of God in such a horrific setting could lead to an understanding of life in wilderness America.

Mary White Rowlandson, *The Sovereignty and Goodness of God ... Being a Narrative of the Captivity and Restauration of Mrs. Mary Rowlandson* (Boston, 1720). Rare Book and Special Collections Division, Library of Congress.

living in the wilderness, but drawing on her belief in God and her reading of the Bible, she was able to resist. Through all these tribulations she came to realize her imperfections and her absolute dependence on God. In time she was rescued and restored to her family, but the captivity experience changed her and gave her a new insight into her relationship with God. Similarly, many of the Puritan settlers found Rowlandson's captivity, together with their own experiences in the wilderness of the New World, gave new meaning to life and new understanding of God's purpose.

Many such captivity narratives were published over the years and several went through multiple editions. It is estimated that between 1677 and 1750 nearly two thousand people were carried off into captivity. Almost everyone knew someone (or had heard of someone) who had been captured. Thus for a time, the captivity narrative served as an effective vehicle for capturing and defining the American experience.

For some, however, the captivity narrative view of the wilderness was too Puritan: it was too dark and too doctrinal. This vision of America did not resonate far beyond New England, and indeed after about 1750 few New Englanders found larger significance in the narratives. Though, as we have seen, captivity narratives such as *The Narrative of the Life of Mrs. Mary Jemison*, published by James Bemis in 1824, continued to attract many readers, their appeal was mainly as tales of adventure rather than as a means of understanding God or the American experience.

The seventeenth-century frontier may have been portrayed as a dark Hell by the Puritans, but for most Americans at the end of the eighteenth century it seemed a bright place of opportunity. There was plenty of land to be claimed, the only problem being that the land was already occupied by Indians or claimed by other Europeans. In spite of these very real impediments to settlement, ultimately nothing could impede the flow of western emigrants. By the 1780s there were already a good many settlers west of the Alleghenies, principally in Kentucky.

One of these was John Filson, who entered Kentucky in 1783. He was a schoolteacher turned surveyor and land speculator. After his

THE
DISCOVERY, SETTLEMENT
And present State of
KENTUCKE:
AND
An ESSAY towards the TOPOGRAPHY, and NATURAL HISTORY of that important Country:

To which is added,

An APPENDIX,
CONTAINING,

I. The ADVENTURES of Col. *Daniel Boon*, one of the firft Settlers, comprehending every important Occurrence in the political Hiftory of that Province.

II The MINUTES of the *Piankafhaw* council, held at *Poft St. Vincents, April* 15, 1784.

III. An ACCOUNT of the *Indian* Nations inhabiting within the Limits of the Thirteen United States, their Manners and Cuftoms, and Reflections on their Origin.

IV. The STAGES and DISTANCES between *Philadelphia* and the Falls of the *Ohio*; from *Pittfburg* to *Penfacola* and feveral other Places. —The Whole illuftrated by a new and accurate MAP of *Kentucke* and the Country adjoining, drawn from actual Surveys.

By JOHN FILSON.

Wilmington, Printed by JAMES ADAMS, 1784.

APPENDIX.

The ADVENTURES of Col. DANIEL BOON; containing a NARRATIVE of the WARS of Kentucke.

CURIOSITY is natural to the foul of man, and interefting objects have a powerful influence on our affections. Let thefe influencing powers actuate, by the permiffion or difpofal of Providence, from felfifh or focial views, yet in time the myfterious will of Heaven is unfolded, and we behold our conduct, from whatfoever motives excited, operating to anfwer the important defigns of heaven. Thus we behold Kentucke, lately an howling wildernefs, the habitation of favages and wild beafts, become a fruitful field ; this region, fo favourably diftinguifhed by nature, now become the habitation of civilization,

G at

A schoolteacher and land speculator, John Filson (ca. 1744–1788) entered Kentucky in 1783, where he met Daniel Boone. Filson and Boone spent many hours conversing while Boone acted as Filson's guide. Much of what Filson learned about Kentucky was from Boone, and when he returned to the East in 1784 to write an account of the territory in the hope of selling land, he decided to add an "autobiography" of Boone as an appendix.

John Filson, *Discovery, Settlement, and Present State of Kentucke* (Wilmington: Printed by James Adams, 1784). Rare Book and Special Collections Division, Library of Congress.

"Curiosity is natural to the soul of man, and interesting objects have a powerful influence on our affections." The opening words of Filson's remarkable account of "The Adventures of Col. Daniel Boon," narrated in Boone's first person, proved to be true for this work. Appended to *Discovery, Settlement, and Present State of Kentucke*, the tale of Boone's life in the wilderness soon was detached and published separately. It achieved enormous worldwide popularity as it was translated into many languages and reprinted again and again.

Opening page, "Appendix: The Adventures of Col. Daniel Boon; Containing a Narrative of the Wars of Kentucke," from John Filson, *Discovery, Settlement, and Present State of Kentucke* (Wilmington: Printed by James Adams, 1784). Rare Book and Special Collections Division, Library of Congress.

"Daniel Boone's First View of Kentucky," a steel engraving by Alfred Jones after a painting by William Ranney (1850), illustrates the mythic Boone, the pathfinder, gazing into the new and fertile land of promise.

Alfred Jones after William T. Ranney, "Daniel Boone's First View of Kentucky," steel engraving, 1850, *American Art–Union Bulletin* 38 (May 1850), 16. Courtesy of the Boston Athenaeum.

return east in 1784, he wrote *The Discovery, Settlement, and Present State of Kentucke*, which was published in Wilmington, Delaware. His book was really an extended real-estate promotion for settlement in Kentucky. As an appendix to the work, Filson included "The Adventures of Col. Daniel Boon."

Filson's book was immediately popular, not as a sales brochure but because of its appendix. Daniel Boone was a figure who captured the reader's attention. For some, particularly for Europeans, his story was interesting because it was exotic, but for many Americans it struck a sympathetic chord. Here was a contemporary man most Americans could identify with. Boone had been Filson's guide on several journeys in Kentucky, but rather than an account of those experiences, Filson's narrative presents a sort of didactic journey in which Boone undergoes a series of initiations into frontier life that give him increasing understanding of the wilderness and its Indian inhabitants. The climax of Filson's account comes after Boone has escaped from Indian captivity, his

only companion having been killed. Alone in the wilderness, Boone suffers "dreadful apprehensions." But then, on a high summit, he looks out over the countryside:

I surveyed the famous river Ohio that rolled in silent dignity, marking the western boundary of Kentucke with inconceivable grandeur. At a vast distance I beheld the mountains lift their venerable brows, and penetrate the clouds. All things were still. I kindled a fire near a fountain of sweet water, and feasted on the loin of a buck, which a few hours before I had killed.

At this moment of epiphany, Daniel Boone sees the land for what it can become. He resolves to bring his family to Kentucky, "which I esteemed a second paradise."

At the end of "The Adventures," Boone has grown in self-knowledge and self-discipline (and has gained an understanding of the design of God) to the point where he can exercise his will and create a utopia out of the wilderness. "Now the scene is changed, peace crowns the sylvan shade. I now live in peace and safety, enjoying the sweets of liberty, and the bounties of Providence, with my once fellow-sufferers, in this delightful country, which I have seen purchased with a vast expense of blood and treasure." For many readers, this was a version of their own story and indeed the story of the entire nation. Here was a vision that resonated at a visceral level for a great many Americans. It was not the dark rejection of the frontier of the Puritans, but an optimistic and opportunistic embrace of the frontier. To be sure the wilderness and its inhabitants were formidable obstacles, but as Boone the hunter had mastered both bears and Indians, so too could the settlers who followed him through the Cumberland Gap master the new environment. In so doing, they would create a new nation.

Filson's whole work, *The Discovery, Settlement, and Present State of Kentucke* (including "The Adventures of Col. Daniel Boon") was translated into French and published in Paris in 1785. In the same year the appendix alone, the *Adventures of Col. Daniel Boon*, was translated into German and published in Frankfort and in a Viennese magazine. Europeans, particularly the French, were much taken with the image of the back-woodsman-hunter Boone, who in Filson's depiction was also part modern philosopher, indeed the epitome of the natural man, able to manage equally well in the simplicity of the prelapsarian wilderness and the complexity of a degenerate modern society. In 1790 the whole work was

A portrait painter in Kentucky and Missouri before he traveled to London to study painting in 1823, Chester Harding painted a portrait of Daniel Boone (1734–1820) near the end of Boone's life. After Boone's death, Harding also completed a full-length portrait of the great man in hunting garb, but in 1861 he destroyed that oil painting.

Chester Harding, *Daniel Boone*, oil on canvas, 1820. Courtesy of the Massachusetts Historical Society (MHS image no. 386).

translated into German and published in Leipzig. It then made its way to London, where it appeared in 1793, both as part of Gilbert Imlay's *Topographical Description of the Western Territory of North America* and as a separate publication. Ten years after Filson first published his book in the small town of Wilmington, Daniel Boone was known across much of the western world.

In the United States, Filson's treatment of Boone was revised in 1786 by John Trumbull, a printer in Norwich, Connecticut. Trumbull removed the philosophical side of Boone that had captured the European imagination, reducing the work by one-third. What remained was Boone, the frontier man of action. Although some might have decried the supposed debasement of Boone's character, Trumbull knew what he was doing. His Boone was less complicated and more comprehensible to the average American reader. As a result, Trumbull had a very profitable book on his hands. It was this version of Filson's *Adventures of Col. Daniel Boon* that was repeatedly reprinted, and this image of Boone became the received version. In 1787 it was reprinted in Mathew Carey's magazine, *American Museum*, which gave it a large readership. In 1794 it was included in *Beer's Almanac*, which again spread the narrative far and wide. Because Trumbull's version was widely reprinted and circulated, the name Daniel Boone became known universally across the United States.

Whatever the factual differences between the truth of Boone's real life in Kentucky and Filson's version in print, Boone himself never contradicted the printed version. Indeed he endorsed the contents of Filson's book as "exceeding good performances, containing as accurate a description of our country as we think can possibly be given." Over the years, Boone never criticized the work. In about 1797, an English traveler, Francis Bailey, happened to come upon Boone on the Ohio River. He called to Boone to leave his canoe and join him on his flatboat. When Bailey realized who his visitor was, he pulled out a copy of Filson and watched Boone's "face brighten up" as he read from the book. Boone then "confirmed all that was there related of him" was true. On another occasion some years later Boone again affirmed, "All true! Every word true! Not a lie in it!"

Boone, then, represents the archetype of the American frontier hero. For him the frontier is a positive place, though certainly a dangerous one. By the very act of facing that danger and creating farms and towns out of the wilderness, Americans created a new and vital nation. Boone died in 1820, an event that stimulated a new version of the narrative that brought Boone's life to closure. This version, which was based on Trumbull's revision, was first issued in 1823 by C. Wilder in Brooklyn, New York: "To which is added, a narration of the most important incidents of his life from the latter period, until the period of his death. . . . Annexed, is an eulogy on Col. Boon and his choice of life, by Lord Byron." The continuation of the life of Boone was written by "a near relation of the colonel (a resident of Cincinnati)." This new version was reprinted by Henry Trumbull in Providence, Rhode Island, in 1824, and then by Wilder again in 1828.

The greatest contribution to the Boone legend was made by Timothy Flint of Cincinnati. Flint, who, as we have already noted, was one of the foremost literary figures in Cincinnati and the West in the 1820s and 1830s, had long been fascinated with Boone. He first wrote about him in detail in his *Condensed Geography and History of the United States, or the Mississippi Valley*, published in Cincinnati 1828. He next recounted Boone's exploits in *Indian Wars of the West*, also published in Cincinnati, in 1833. But it was his *Biographical Memoir of Daniel Boone, the First Settler of Kentucky: Interspersed with Incidents in the Early Annals of the Country*, published in Cincinnati in the same year, that has forever linked Flint's name to the great frontier hunter and pathfinder. Flint methodically took Filson's account of Boone, in all its variations, any published or newspaper accounts he could find, and oral recollections and legends as the basis for his biographical treatment. He even visited Boone in his final years in Missouri.

Timothy Flint viewed Boone as the archetypal frontiersman. In *Indian Wars* he wrote of Boone:

He stands at the head of a remarkable class of people, almost new in the history of the species, trained by circumstances to a singular and unique character, and in many respects dissimilar to that of the first settlers on the shores of the Atlantic. The thoughts of these backwoodsmen expatiated with delight, only when they were in a boundless forest, filled with game, with a pack of dogs behind them, and a rifle on their shoulders. Yet as much as their character seems dashed with a wild recklessness, they were as generally remarkable for high notions of honor and generosity, as for hardihood, endurance, and bravery.

This is Boone the self-made man, owing nothing to heredity or tradition. His story is one of initiation into the life of the hunter and pathfinder, a life that Flint regards as inherently western. So for Flint and his many readers, Boone was the American Everyman who epitomized and defined the American national character. In Boone's life as a hunter and pathfinder, Flint sees the American nation's identity.

When Flint's *Biographical Memoir of Daniel Boone* was first published by the Cincinnati firm of N. and G. Guilford, it consisted of 252 pages and included woodcut illustrations. The work was stereotyped, thus allowing it to be easily reprinted from the plates as demand warranted. And indeed, demand warranted that it be reprinted many times. In 1835, N. and G. Guildford issued a reprint. In 1836, George Conclin had possession of the plates and he prepared another Cincinnati printing. Over the next ten years, Conclin reprinted the work eight more times. In 1847, a new title page was made, *The First White Man of the West; or, The Life and Exploits of Colonel Daniel Boone, the First Settler of Kentucky; Interspersed with Incidents in the Early Annals of the Country*, which may have given the impression that this was a revised edition, but in fact the original plates continued to be used. Conclin printed this "new" edition in 1847 and again in 1849.

The book was printed by others in Cincinnati as well: by Anderson, Gates & Wright in 1847 and 1858; by E. Morgan in 1850; by H. S. J. Applegate & Company in 1851 and 1856; and by H. M. Rulison (and D. Rulison, Philadelphia) in 1856. After a hiatus of ten years a "new edition" appeared in Cincinnati in 1868, published by U. P. James. This edition, now titled *The Life and Adventures of Daniel Boone, the First Settler of Kentucky: Interspersed with Incidents in the Early Annals of the Country*, was in fact no different from Flint's original, except for an additional few pages at the end, "an account of Captain Estill's defeat" in 1782 in Kentucky.

There followed many subsequent variations and versions of the frontier hero, both historical and literary. Almost every one derived in some way from Daniel Boone. Each subsequent frontier hero was defined against Boone's image, and this was no less true of Davy Crockett. Crockett was born in 1786 in east Tennessee, two years after Filson published Boone's *Adventures*. In 1811 his family moved west, eventually ending up in the west Tennessee woodlands with which his name later became associated. Crockett hunted, and he fought Indians under Andrew Jackson. In 1821 he was elected to the state legislature and then served in U.S. Congress in Washington for three terms.

Crockett was a storyteller, and stories were a vital part of his political success. He would capture his listeners' attention, relax them with a good yarn, and then drive home his moral. It was a technique put to good use some years later by another backwoods politician, Abraham Lincoln. But even when he was at a loss for words, Crockett had an uncanny ability to salvage the situation:

I got up and told the people, I reckoned they know'd what I come for, but if not, I could tell them. I had come for their votes, and if they didn't watch mighty close, I'd get them too. But the worst of all was, that I couldn't tell them anything about government. I tried to speak about something, and I cared very little what, until I choked up as bad as if my mouth had been jam'd and cram'd chock full of dry mush. There the people stood, listening all the while, with their eyes, mouths, and years all open, to catch every word I would speak.

At last I told them I was like a fellow I had heard of not long before. He was beating on the head of an empty barrel near the road-side, when a traveler, who was passing along, asked him what he was doing that for? The fellow replied, that there was some cider in that barrel a few days before, and he was trying to see if there was any then but if there was he couldn't get at it. I told them that there had been a little bit of a speech in me a while ago, but I believed I couldn't get it. . . . I took care to remark that I was as dry as a powder horn, and I thought it was time for us all to wet our whistles a little; and so I put off to the liquor stand, and was followed by the greater part of the crowd.

Crockett's public persona of the buckskin-clad hunter topped by a coonskin cap derived in some part from a portrait of Daniel Boone made by Chester Harding in 1820 just before Boone's death. Harding soon made a full-length version that was copied as an engraving by James Otto Lewis, who then employed an actor and musician, Noah Ludlow, to gild frames

Davy Crockett shown in a frontispiece portrait to his *Account of Col. Crockett's Tour to the North and Down East* (1835) looks little different from any of his other fellow congressmen. Though Crockett often sounded like a wild frontiersman in his public speeches, he did not look the part.

"David Crockett," frontispiece portrait from Davy Crockett, *Account of Col. Crockett's Tour to the North and Down East* (Philadelphia: E. L. Carey and A. Hart, 1835). Rare Book and Special Collections Division, Library of Congress.

for the engraving. The actor Ludlow took away with him the image of Boone the hunter in buckskin and moccasins, carrying a long rifle, with his beaver hat. A couple of years later, Ludlow was in New Orleans, where he appeared as a hunter to sing the song "The Hunters of Kentucky," written by S. W. Woodworth, which celebrated the American victory over the British in the Battle of New Orleans. He dressed exactly like Boone in Lewis's engraving except, unable to find the right beaver hat, he substituted a coonskin cap. He appeared on stage singing:

> *We are a hardy freeborn race,*
> *Each man to fear a stranger,*
> *Whate'er the game, we join in chase,*
> *Despising toil and danger;*
> *And if a daring foe annoys,*
> *Whate'er his strength and forces,*
> *We'll show him that Kentucky boys*
> *Are "alligator horses."*
> *O Kentucky, the hunters of Kentucky.*
> *O Kentucky, the hunters of Kentucky.*

While singing the rousing chorus, Ludlow pointed his rifle at the audience and threw his coonskin cap. This brought the house down.

The performance was a huge success, and Ludlow repeated it for many years. His portrayal of the Old Kentucky Hunter in buckskins and coonskin cap was firmly established as a stock image, and as Crockett began to gain national exposure he consciously adopted this persona. This image was reinforced when a stage melodrama by James Kirke Paulding, *The Lion of the West*, opened in New York for a very successful run in the early 1830s. The play featured a Kentucky backwoodsman turned congressman, Nimrod Wildfire, who was modeled on Crockett to some degree, and as this image of the backwoodsman gained currency, Crockett took it, too, as his own. Davy Crockett was well on his way to becoming a national figure in politics and legend.

Crockett's repertoire of stories, *The Life and Adventures of Colonel David Crockett of West Tennessee* (also known as *Sketches and Eccentricities of Col. David Crockett*), first made it into print in Cincinnati in 1833 in the heat of his election campaign against William Fitzgerald to reclaim his former seat in Congress. This work was secretly written by James Strange French, who drew upon stories told him by Matthew St. Clair Clarke, clerk of the House of Representatives, and others. It was an odd combination of tall tales that at times portrayed Crockett as a rural simpleton far out of his depth in politics and at others portrayed him as the consummate hunter. Whatever the effect of the book on the election, Crockett prevailed, but he was furious about the publication of *Sketches and Eccentricities*.

Crockett then decided to write his own version of his story, *A Narrative of the Life of David Crockett of the State of Tennessee*, which was published in 1834 by Carey and Hart in Philadelphia. This narrative was written with the assistance of Thomas Chilton, a congressman from Kentucky and Crockett's close friend, as Crockett recounted in a letter of February 3, 1834, to his son: "I am ingaged in writing of my life and I have completed one hundred and ten pages and I have Mr Chlton to correct it as I write it. . . . I may take a trip through the eastern States during the recess of Congress and Sell the Book . . . a great many have preswaded me . . . that my presents [i.e., presence] will make thousands of people buy my book."

In fact, the whole manuscript delivered to Carey and Hart was in Chilton's hand, and it may well be that Chilton wrote the book as Crockett supplied the subject material. Though far less boisterous and boastful than *Sketches and Eccentricities*, it nonetheless emphasized that hallmark of the Crockett myth, the hunt. For Crockett, the act of hunting was the defining act of the frontiersman:

I pursued on, but my other hunters . . . killed the bear before I got up with him. I gave him to them, and cut out again for a creek called Big Clover, which wa'n't very far off. Just as I got there, and was entering a cane brake, my dogs all broke and went ahead. . . . I listened awhile and found my dogs was in two companies, and that both was in a snorting fight. I sent my little son to one and I broke for t'other. I got to mine first, and found my dogs had a two-year-old bear down, a-wooling away on him, so I just took out my big butcher, and went up and slap'd

The hunt was an important part of Crockett's life, and he claimed to have killed more bears than any other contemporary hunter. This aspect of his life was taken over intact into the legend.

Bear fight, *Crockett Almanac* 1836, Nashville, Tenn. (i.e., Boston), p. 29. Rare Book and Special Collections Division, Library of Congress.

it into him, and killed him without shooting. . . . In a short time, I heard my little son fire at his bear; when I went to him he had killed it too. . . . We pushed on . . . and . . . found that we had a still larger bear than either of them we had killed, treed by himself. We killed that one also, which made three we had killed in less than half an hour.

Crockett's hopes for huge sales were well founded. The book in 1834 alone went through at least five printings in Philadelphia, in addition to printings in Cincinnati, Baltimore, Boston, and London. By 1837, it was in its "24th edition."

Crockett, however, had become enmeshed in political difficulties, and many of his supporters refused to vote for him in the next election. He said that if his constituents did not reelect him, they could go to Hell and he would go to Texas. And so, defeated in the election and repudiated by his constituents, Crockett and several close companions set out for Texas on November 1, 1835. Crockett's part in the siege of the Alamo has become an essential element in Texas mythology, and needs no recounting here. In one version of that drama, Crockett was captured and his execution ordered by the Mexican general Santa Anna, and it soon became common knowledge that the unarmed hunter had been cut down while springing like a tiger for Santa Anna's throat.

In death, Crockett's fame was assured. His Philadelphia publisher, Carey and Hart, immediately saw the potential in Crockett's glorious demise, and they arranged for Richard Penn Smith to write *Col. Crockett's Exploits and Adventures in Texas Wherein Is Contained a Full Account of his Journey from Tennessee to the Red River and Natchitoches, and Thence across Texas to San Antonio, Including His Many Hair-Breadth Escapes together with a Topographical, Historical, and Political View of Texas, Written by Himself; the Narrative Brought Down from the Death of Col. Crockett to the Battle of San Jacinto, by an Eyewitness.* Smith's authorship was carefully hidden, and it was reported that this was Crockett's diary, which had been found in the ruins by one Charles T. Beale, who had sent it to Alex J. Dumas for publication.

Carey and Hart had the book published under the imprint of T. K. and P. G. Collins, and it sold more than ten thousand copies in its first year. As an added bonus, Carey and Hart were able to sell all their warehoused copies of *An Account of Col. Crockett's Tour to the North and Down East*, which had appeared the year before with very weak sales. Crockett's death gave new life even to this book, and by 1837 it was in its tenth printing. It seemed anything associated with Davy Crockett was sure to sell.

Popular even before Crockett's death, the most well known of the publications that featured the tall tales of the braggart Crockett had been the *Crockett Almanac*, which first appeared in 1835. Though bearing an imprint that proclaimed that the almanacs were published in Nashville, they were actually produced in Boston. Before his death, they claimed to have been written by Crockett himself, and then by the heirs of Crockett, until finally in 1838, any direct connection to Crockett disappeared. Other *Crockett Almanacs* followed in the 1840s, openly published in Boston, New York, Philadelphia, Baltimore, and Albany. Like all almanacs, these contained practical information on agriculture, the weather, and so forth, but most of all they featured tall tales concerned with Crockett, and others such as Kit Carson or Mike Fink.

The *Crockett Almanacs* were largely responsible for Crockett's contribution to the frontier myth. Here we find the braggart:

Congress allows lemonade to the members and has it charged under the head of stationery—I move also that whiskey be allowed under the item of fuel. For bitters I can suck away at a noggin of aquafortis, sweetened with brimstone, stirred with a lightning rod, and skimmed with a hurricane. I've soaked my head and shoulders

Soon after Crockett's death, his image had completed its transformation. Here we see the Davy Crockett of legend in buckskins, long rifle, and skin cap. In this instance, Crockett is wearing a wildcat-skin cap, clearly modeled on the widely available engraving of fictional Nimrod Wildfire in the play *Lion of the West* (who himself was based on the real Crockett of the late 1820s).

Front cover, *Crockett Almanac* 1837, Nashville, Tenn. (i.e., Boston). Rare Book and Special Collections Division, Library of Congress.

in Salt River so much that I'm always corned. I can walk like an ox, run like a fox, swim like an eel, yell like an Indian, fight like the devil, spout like an earthquake, [and] make love like a mad bull.

This braggadocio version of Crockett appealed to those, like himself, who were plain-spoken and skilled in hunting, fighting, and gambling. Indeed, Crockett was very popular with the less sophisticated reader across the entire country. This Crockett was racist, crude, xenophobic, and utterly opposed to all Indians: "I never will be revenged till I've extinctified the whole race of varmints. . . . No human ever hated an Injun more than Davy Crockett." For those who viewed the frontier as a place of unlimited resources to be exploited and its native inhabitants as implacable foes to be exterminated, Crockett was a hero to be emulated.

One contemporary image of Daniel Boone exhibited these same qualities, particularly the mindless hatred of Indians. John A. McClung's *Sketches of Western Adventure* appeared in 1832, published in Maysville, Kentucky, by L. Collins and also in Philadelphia by Griggs & Elliot. McClung's Boone was cut from the same racist cloth as was Crockett. This Boone found the idea of negotiating with Indians as equals to be ludicrous and repugnant. Instead, he desired nothing more than the "thrilling excitement of savage warfare." It proved to be a popular work—though not as popular as Flint's contemporary treatment—and was reprinted in Cincinnati four more times during the 1830s by the firm of J. A. James (later U. P. James). In the 1840s, it was published in Dayton, Ohio, by Ellis & Clafin, and by 1879 it had gone through thirteen printings.

By the 1850s the frontier had shifted westward and the nation's attention focused on new heroes. Daniel Boone and Davy Crockett did not disappear, but other figures were now more often associated with the frontier.

Kit Carson came to national attention in the 1840s, when he served as John C. Frémont's guide on several expeditions throughout the West. He first appeared as the subject of a novel in 1849 with the publication of Charles A. Averill's *Kit Carson: The Prince of Gold Hunters.* Carson bears no resemblance to Crockett or the braggart frontier hero. He is more like Filson's Boone, an individual who exhibits a natural nobility; who knows no fear; and who possesses an indomitable spirit.

Carson, the former mountain man clad in buckskin, forms a link between the backwoodsman of Kentucky or Tennessee and the plainsman typified by Buffalo Bill Cody. With the advent of the dime novel in 1860, Carson was featured in more than seventy titles during the next thirty years, but he never really caught on. In the post–Civil War period, the figure who indisputably popularized the frontier hero was Buffalo Bill Cody.

Buffalo Bill has long suffered from a reputation that he has not deserved. Because he was a successful showman, many have assumed that his frontier hero persona was nothing more than an act. William Cody will always be something of an enigma, but his real accomplishments as a frontier hero are undeniable. Born in 1846 in Iowa, young William grew up in Kansas during the time when that territory was known as "Bloody Kansas." His father was an ardent abolitionist, who settled his family in Salt Creek Valley, three miles west of Fort Leavenworth. As luck would have it, Salt Creek Valley was settled mostly by proslavery Missourians. When pressed to express an opinion in 1854, Isaac Cody stated his antislavery views and as a result was stabbed in the chest. Though the wound was not fatal, Isaac Cody never regained good health and died on April 21, 1857. Isaac Cody's death left Mary Cody with young Bill, now the man of the family, four daughters, and a baby son. Unable to support the family by taking in borders, Mary Cody was forced to send the eleven-year-old boy out to find work. He managed to find a job as a messenger for Russell, Majors & Waddell, a freight company in Leaven-

In the dramatic pose on the cover of a dime novel published in 1873, Daniel Boone wears the trademark coonskin cap of the frontier huntsman: he as been transformed into Davy Crockett.

Front cover, Frederick Whittaker, *Boone, the Hunter; or, The Backwoods Belle* (1873). Beadle's Dime Novels, no. 278. Rare Book and Special Collections Division, Library of Congress.

worth, Kansas. He subsequently worked as a bullwhacker on a wagon train to Ft. Laramie, and then in 1859 he joined the Pike's Peak gold rush, only to return home broke. At the age of thirteen he spent the winter trapping beaver in central Kansas along the Republican River. It was during this winter that the incident of his breaking a leg and being holed up for over a month, recounted earlier, occurred.

The first Buffalo Bill dime novel, *Buffalo Bill, the King of Border Men*, was written by Ned Buntline and serialized in the *New York Weekly* in 1869. Buntline often figures prominently when Buffalo Bill dime novels are mentioned, but in fact only four original novels carry his name. Their most significant and influential author was Colonel Prentiss Ingraham. A close associate of the real Buffalo Bill, Ingraham wrote more than one hundred of the dime novels, though never using his own name.

Ned Buntline, "Buffalo Bill: The King of Border Men," *New York Weekly* 25, no. 6 (December 23, 1869). Library of Congress (microfilm 38028).

In 1860 or 1861 Bill Cody is reputed to have ridden for the Pony Express, but this claim remains a point of some controversy. In any case, at the outbreak of the Civil War, Cody was too young to enlist, so he joined a Jayhawker band of antislavery guerrilla irregulars raiding into Missouri. When he turned eighteen he enlisted in the Seventh Kansas Cavalry and saw action in northern Mississippi at the battle of Tupelo in 1864 and then in Missouri in September and October of that year. After the war he married and attempted to settle down, but this proved impossible. In 1866 and 1867, he found employment as a scout, guide, and dispatch bearer for the army in Kansas. In 1867 and 1868, he worked for the Kansas Pacific Railroad as a hunter. It was here that Cody became known as Buffalo Bill, a tribute to his prowess. In 1868, at the age of twenty-two, Cody was appointed chief of scouts for the U.S. Fifth Cavalry, and in 1872 he was awarded the Congressional Medal of Honor in recognition of his actions as scout in the Indian wars.

The name of Buffalo Bill was becoming widely known on the plains, but it was the arrival in Fort McPherson in 1869 of E. Z. C. Judson, better known by the pseudonym Ned Buntline, who decided to use Bill as the subject for his next dime novel, that brought the hunter's name before the whole world. On Monday, December 13, of that year, the *Baltimore American* was one of several newspapers that headlined "Ned Buntline's Great Story! The Great Living Scout! Buffalo Bill, The King of Border Men! The Wildest, Truest Story Ned Buntline ever Wrote." This first installment ended with the villain, M'Kandlas, addressing his band of ruffians: "We'll then wipe out Buffalo Bill and his party, and make a raid down the river as far as we can and then strike for the Platte for a rest." At this exciting moment Buntline ended the installment and announced, "The continuation of this wild, true and exciting story will be found in the *New York Weekly*, No. 7, which can be purchased from all News Agents on and after Tuesday, December 14th."

Buntline wrote a compelling action-filled tale that hooked his readers in the first installment. Though it was wild and exciting, as Cody's life actually was, there was little truth in this account of Buffalo Bill, which unfortunately set the standard for subsequent novels. The character of Buffalo Bill had only a tenuous connection with the real Buffalo Bill. But there was something about the fictional Buffalo Bill that caught the public's attention and held it.

More dime novels were written about Buffalo Bill than about any other

Buffalo Bill's Wild West was intended to be the real thing and not staged. And so it was received by countless spectators from 1883 until Cody's death in 1917. Posters advertising the "show" appeared across the nation and, combined with dime novel covers, made the image of Buffalo Bill as well known as that of Washington or Lincoln.

Buffalo Bill's Wild West and Congress of Rough Riders of the World. Color lithograph, copyright 1899 by Courier Litho. Co., Buffalo, N.Y. Prints and Photographs Division, Library of Congress (LC-USZ62-1161).

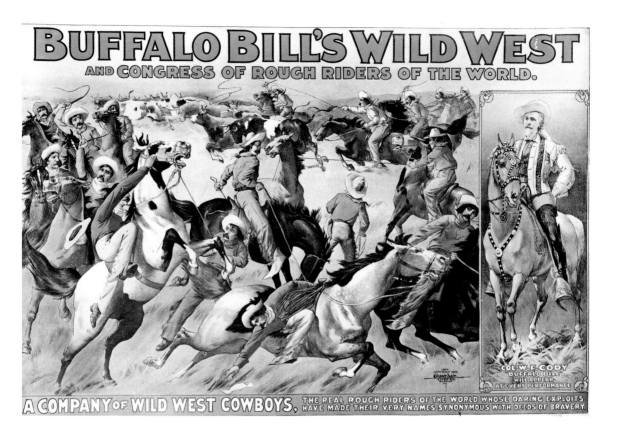

frontier hero. Some 557 novels featured Buffalo Bill, and when we include reprints—the stories tended to be recycled with new titles every ten years—the total comes to 1,700 different titles in the United States alone. Several hundred more were published in England, Germany, Italy, Spain, France, Sweden, Denmark, and elsewhere. All told, these novels amounted to more than twenty-five million words devoted to Buffalo Bill. Out of all of these volumes, twenty-two were signed by Buffalo Bill, and on balance it seems likely he was indeed the author of some of them. Up until the 1890s only a few of these novels would appear annually, but after Buffalo Bill's Wild West began in 1883 the pace increased. Reflecting the Wild West's immense popularity, the number of novels published increased to twenty-three in 1896.

In 1901 the publishing house of Street and Smith launched a weekly *Buffalo Bill Stories* (and later *New Buffalo Bill Weekly*) and soon there were hardly any children, or any adults, in America who were not inspired by the exploits of Buffalo Bill. The back cover of each issue stated: "Buffalo Bill is more popular today than he ever was, and, consequently, everybody ought to know all there is to know about him. In no manner can you become so thoroughly acquainted with the actual habits and life of this great man, as by reading the *New Buffalo Bill Weekly*." Ned Buntline's first Buffalo Bill novel had been published in Street and Smith's *New York Weekly*, and it seems only fitting that the publisher's *Buffalo Bill Stories* were to be the vehicle that would ensure the frontier scout's eternal fame.

Buntline's Buffalo Bill owed much to the previous images of Boone and Crockett, as the backwoods hero. He spoke in ungrammatical English but nonetheless exhibited an interior nobility that allowed him to win and marry the damsel he rescued from a band of drunken soldiers. This was to be the first and only time Buffalo Bill had a love interest in all the novels. But Buntline only wrote four Buffalo Bill novels. It was Prentiss Ingraham, a close associate of Cody's

Although Buffalo Bill and his pards rode hard they were too late. Rounding a bend in the trail, they came suddenly upon the burning ammunition wagon.

and author of about 120 Buffalo Bill novels, who really created the fictional character of Buffalo Bill.

Ingraham's Buffalo Bill shed his buckskin, his ungrammatical English, his humorous demeanor, and his awkwardness in social situations. Replacing the stock backwoodsman, Ingraham's hero was a "prince of the plains." His natural nobility was evident in his flawless demeanor, his social bearing, and his unwavering commitment to the highest ideals. To some degree, we had come full circle to return to Filson's Boone, whose inner nobility was now fully externalized, though there was a shallowness to the static Buffalo Bill that remained unequal to the depth and dynamism of Filson's philosophical frontier hunter. Ironically, the historical Buffalo Bill had a complexity and dynamism comparable to Boone's, which his fictional persona could never match.

Whatever the literary merits of these Buffalo Bill novels and despite the stunted character development of their frontier hero, the novels were spectacularly successful in spreading the popular image of the frontier and

Beginning in 1901, the New York publisher Street and Smith started a weekly series of dime novels featuring Buffalo Bill (which actually cost a nickel). Closely tied to the Wild West show, the series featured the "two Bills" after Buffalo Bill and Pawnee Bill merged their western shows at the end of the 1908 season. Each novel had an alternate title, the first part featuring Buffalo Bill and the second part featuring Pawnee Bill, and each was signed "by the Author of Buffalo Bill."

Buffalo Bill's Merry War, or, Pawnee Bill's Pawnee Pard, The Buffalo Bill Stories Devoted to Far West Life, no. 527 (New York: Street and Smith, June 17, 1911). Courtesy of the Department of Special Collections, Kenneth Spencer Research Library, University of Kansas.

its values throughout virtually every part of American society from 1870 to 1930. From that popular image of the frontier has come a national vision of the United States that transcends the geographical limitations of its origin. As the factual frontier of the West has receded in history, the vision of a mythical frontier has expanded to encompass all parts of the nation. This idea of the frontier, espousing hard-working individualism and an optimistic "can-do" attitude, has become a powerful theme in American life. Indeed, as a result, the word frontier has taken on a positive meaning indicating a new and challenging field or area of knowledge to be conquered. John F. Kennedy understood this very well when he called his legislative program the "New Frontier."

When a nation's historical vision is exposed as myth, it loses its power. If there is no new vision to replace the old, a nation may decline and lose its way, as happened in England when the idea of the nation's Anglo-Saxon origin was shown to be myth. The moral justification for the British Empire was thereby greatly diminished, and with the loss of empire, England seemed a nation adrift without a unifying national vision.

In America, the myth of frontier values, now transformed into the national and even universal vision of the "American Dream," still resonates at a visceral level and remains a powerful interpretation of the American experience. Though historians may argue about the role of the frontier hero, or the frontier itself, in shaping the American nation, Americans themselves have never been so reluctant or particular. Frederick Jackson Turner's frontier thesis in its popular form has been embodied by the fictional personae of Daniel Boone, Davy Crockett, Kit Carson, and Buffalo Bill Cody in countless popular narratives, stories, legends, and dime novels. Through the medium of the printed page, the nation found its collective vision in the nineteenth century. Just as American frontier heroes were transformed in the popular press in the early twentieth century into national icons that embodied a sense of collective identity, these mythic characters were perpetuated in new forms of popular mass media in the second half of the twentieth century. Though many segments of contemporary American society no longer identify with the frontier, the overarching vision of America as a nation of opportunity continues to epitomize the American experience.

Buffalo Bill remains an enigmatic figure today, a combination of frontier scout and circus showman, but to his contemporaries he embodied the mythic West.

Buffalo Bill Cody, photograph, 1903. Prints and Photographs Division, Library of Congress (LC-USZ62-111880).

FURTHER READING

Athearn, Robert G. *The Mythic West in Twentieth-Century America*. Lawrence: University Press of Kansas, 1986.

Billington, Ray Allen. *Land of Savagery, Land of Promise: The European Image of the American Frontier in the Nineteenth Century*. New York: Norton, 1981.

———. *The Genesis of the Frontier Thesis: A Study in Historical Creativity*. San Marino: Huntington Library, 1971.

Billington, Ray Allen, and Martin Ridge. *Westward Expansion: A History of the American Frontier*. Albuquerque: University of New Mexico Press, 2001.

Bold, Christine. *Selling the Wild West: Popular Western Fiction*. Bloomington: Indiana University Press, 1987.

Boone, Nathan. *My Father, Daniel Boone: The Draper Interviews with Nathan Boone*. Lexington: University Press of Kentucky, 1999.

Bridger, Bobby. *Buffalo Bill and Sitting Bull: Inventing the Wild West*. Austin: University of Texas Press, 2002.

Brodhead, Richard C. *Cultures of Letters: Scenes of Reading and Writing in Nineteenth-Century America*. Chicago: University of Chicago Press, 1993.

Brown, Bill. *Reading the West: An Anthology of Dime Westerns*. Boston: Bedford Books, 1997.

Brown, Richard D. *Knowledge Is Power: The Diffusion of Information in Early America, 1700–1865*. Oxford: Oxford University Press, 1989.

Bruccoli, Matthew, ed. *The Profession of Authorship in America, 1800–1878*. Columbus: Ohio State University Press, 1968.

Carter, Robert A. *Buffalo Bill Cody: The Man Behind the Legend*. New York: Wiley, 2000.

Cawelti, John. *Adventure, Mystery, and Romance*. Chicago: University of Chicago Press, 1976.

Charvat, William. *Literary Publishing in America, 1790–1850*. Philadelphia: University of Pennsylvania Press, 1959.

Clement, Richard W. *The Book in America: With Images from the Library of Congress.* Golden, Colo.: Fulcrum, 1996.

Colbert, David. *Eyewitness to the American West: From the Aztec Empire to the Digital Frontier in the Words of Those Who Saw It Happen.* New York: Viking, 1998.

Davis, William C. *The American Frontier: Pioneers, Settlers, and Cowboys, 1800–1899.* Norman: University of Oklahoma Press, 1999.

———. *Three Roads to the Alamo: The Lives and Fortunes of David Crockett, James Bowie, and William Barret Travis.* New York: HarperCollins Publishers, 1998.

Denning, Michael. *Mechanic Accents: Dime Novels and Working-Class Culture in America.* New York: Verso, 1987.

Derr, Mark. *The Frontiersman: The Real Life and Many Legends of Davy Crockett.* New York: W. Morrow, 1993.

Dickerson, Donna L. *The Course of Tolerance: Freedom of the Press in Nineteenth-Century America.* Westport, Conn.: Greenwood Press, 1990.

Etulain, Richard W. *Telling Western Stories: From Buffalo Bill to Larry McMurtry.* Albuquerque: University of New Mexico Press, 1999.

———, ed. *Does the Frontier Experience Make America Exceptional?* Boston: Bedford/St. Martin's, 1999.

Faragher, John Mack. *Daniel Boone: The Life and Legend of an American Pioneer.* New York: Henry Holt, 1992.

Gallop, Alan. *Buffalo Bill's British Wild West.* Stroud, Gloucestershire, U.K.: Sutton Pub., 2001.

Georgi-Findlay, Brigitte. *The Frontiers of Women's Writing: Women's Narratives and the Rhetoric of Westward Expansion.* Tucson: University of Arizona Press, 1996.

Gilmore, William J. *Reading Becomes a Necessity of Life: Material and Cultural Life in Rural New England, 1780–1835.* Knoxville: University of Tennessee Press, 1989.

Gilreath, James. "American Book Distribution." *Proceedings of the American Antiquarian Society* 95 (1985): 501–83.

Goetzmann, William H., and William N. Goetzmann. *The West of the Imagination.* New York: Norton, 1986.

Green, James N. *Mathew Carey, Publisher and Patriot.* Philadelphia: Library Company of Philadelphia, 1985.

Hackenberg, Michael, ed. *Getting the Books Out: Papers of the Chicago Conference on the Book in 19th-Century America.* Washington: Center for the Book, Library of Congress, 1987.

Hall, Roger A. *Performing the American Frontier, 1870–1906.* Cambridge and New York: Cambridge University Press, 2001.

Hamilton, Milton. *The Country Printer: New York State, 1785–1830.* Port Washington, N.Y.: I. J. Friedman, 1964.

Hart, James D. *The Popular Book: A History of America's Literary Taste.* New York: Oxford University Press, 1950.

Hasselstrom, Linda M., Gaydell M. Collier, and Nancy Curtis. *Leaning into the Wind: Women Write from the Heart of the West.* Boston: Houghton Mifflin, 1997.

Hauck, Richard Boyd. *Crockett, a Bio-Bibliography.* Westport, Conn.: Greenwood Press, 1982.

Hine, Robert V., and John Mack Faragher. *The American West: A New Interpretive History.* New Haven, Conn.: Yale University Press, 2000.

Jeffrey, Julie Roy. *Frontier Women: "Civilizing" the West? 1840–1880.* New York: Hill and Wang, 1998.

Jones, Daryl. *The Dime Novel Western.* Bowling Green: Popular Press, 1978.

Kaser, David. *Joseph Charless: Printer in the Western Country.* Philadelphia: University of Pennsylvania Press, 1963.

———. *Messrs. Carey & Lea of Philadelphia: A Study in the History of the Booktrade.* Philadelphia: University of Pennsylvania Press, 1957

Kasson, Joy S. *Buffalo Bill's Wild West: Celebrity, Memory, and Popular History.* New York: Hill and Wang, 2000.

Klein, Kerwin Lee. *Frontiers of Historical Imagination: Narrating the European Conquest of Native America, 1890–1990.* Berkeley: University of California Press, 1997.

Klein, Marcus. *Easterns, Westerns, and Private Eyes: American Matters, 1870–1900.* Madison: University of Wisconsin Press, 1994.

Kowalewski, Michael. *Reading the West: New Essays on the Literature of the American West.* Cambridge: New York, 1996.

Lamar, Howard Roberts. *The New Encyclopedia of the American West.* New Haven, Conn.: Yale University Press, 1998.

Lape, Noreen Groover. *West of the Border: The Multicultural Literature of the Western American Frontiers.* Athens: Ohio University Press, 2000.

Lawlor, Mary. *Recalling the Wild: Naturalism and the Closing of the American West.* New Brunswick, N.J.: Rutgers University Press, 2000.

Lehman-Haupt, Hellmut. *The Book in America: A History of the Making and Selling of Books in the United States.* New York: R. R. Bowker, 1951.

Limerick, Patricia Nelson. *The Legacy of Conquest: The Unbroken Past of the American West.* New York: Norton, 1987.

Lofaro, Michael A. *Davy Crockett's Riproarious Shemales and Sentimental Sisters: Women's Tall Tales from the Crockett Almanacs, 1835–1856.* Mechanicsburg, Pa.: Stackpole Books, 2001.

——. *The Life and Adventures of Daniel Boone.* Lexington: University Press of Kentucky, 1978.

——, ed. *Davy Crockett: The Man, the Legend, the Legacy, 1786–1986.* Knoxville: University of Tennessee Press, 1985.

Lofaro, Michael A., and Joe Cummings, eds. *Crockett at Two Hundred: New Perspectives on the Man and the Myth.* Knoxville: University of Tennessee Press, 1989.

Miller, Susan Cummins, ed. *A Sweet, Separate Intimacy: Women Writers of the American Frontier, 1800–1922.* Salt Lake City: University of Utah Press, 2000.

Moylan, Michele, and Lane Stiles, eds. *Reading Books: Essays on the Material Text and Literature in America.* Amherst: University of Massachusetts Press, 1996.

Murdoch, David Hamilton. *The American West: The Invention of a Myth.* Reno: University of Nevada Press, 2001.

Nash, Roderick. *Wilderness and the American Mind.* New Haven, Conn.: Yale University Press, 1967.

Nugent, Walter T. K. *Into the West: The Story of Its People.* New York: A. A. Knopf, 1999.

Parkman, Francis Jr. *The Oregon Trail.* Edited and with an introduction by Bernard Rosenthal. New York: Oxford University Press, 1996.

Peavy, Linda S. *Pioneer Women: The Lives of Women on the Frontier.* Norman: University of Oklahoma Press, 1998.

Peavy, Linda S., and Ursula Smith. *Pioneer Women: The Lives of Women on the Frontier.* New York: Smithmark, 1996.

Remer, Rosalind. *Printers and Men of Capital: Philadelphia Book Publishers in the New Republic.* Philadelphia: University of Pennsylvania Press, 1996.

Ritchie, Robert C., and Paul Andrew Hutton. *Frontier and Region: Essays in Honor of Martin Ridge.* San Marino, Calif.: Huntington Library Press, 1997.

Roberts, Brian. *American Alchemy: The California Gold Rush and Middle-Class Culture.* Chapel Hill: University of North Carolina Press, 2000.

Ronda, James P. *Finding the West: Explorations with Lewis and Clark*. Albuquerque: University of New Mexico Press, 2001.

Rosa, Joseph G. *Wild Bill Hickok: The Man and His Myth*. Lawrence: University Press of Kansas, 1996.

Rourke, Constance. *Davy Crockett*. Lincoln: University of Nebraska Press, 1998.

Rubin, Joan Shelley. *The Making of Middlebrow Culture*. Chapel Hill: University of North Carolina Press, 1992.

Russell, Don. *The Lives and Legends of Buffalo Bill*. Norman: University of Oklahoma Press, 1960.

Sagala, Sandra K. *Buffalo Bill, Actor: A Chronicle of Cody's Theatrical Career*. Bowie, Md.: Heritage Books, 2002.

Shackford, James Atkins. *David Crockett: The Man and the Legend*. Edited by John B. Shackford. Chapel Hill: University of North Carolina Press, 1956.

Silver, Rollo G. *The American Printer, 1787–1825*. Charlottesville: University Press of Virginia for the Bibliographical Society of the University of Virginia, 1967.

Slotkin, Richard. *Gunfighter Nation: The Myth of the Frontier in Twentieth-Century America*. New York: Atheneum, 1992.

———. *The Fatal Environment: The Myth of the Frontier in the Age of Industrialization, 1800–1890*. New York: Atheneum, 1985.

———. *Regeneration through Violence: The Mythology of the American Frontier, 1600–1860*. Middletown, Conn.: Wesleyan University Press, 1973.

Smith, Henry Nash. *Virgin Land: The American West as Symbol and Myth*. Cambridge, Mass.: Harvard University Press, 1950.

Snodgrass, Mary Ellen. *Encyclopedia of Frontier Literature*. Oxford and New York: Oxford University Press, 1999.

Steckmesser, Kent Ladd. *The Western Hero in History and Legend*. Norman: University of Oklahoma Press, 1997.

Stern, Madelein B. *Imprints on History: Book Publishers and American Frontiers*. New York: AMS Press, 1975.

Streeby, Shelley. *American Sensations: Class, Empire, and the Production of Popular Culture*. Berkeley: University of California Press, 2002.

Sutton, Walter. *The Western Book Trade: Cincinnati as a Nineteenth-Century Publishing and Book-trade Center*. Columbus: Ohio State University Press for the Ohio Historical Society, 1961.

Sweeney, J. Gray. *The Columbus of the Woods: Daniel Boone and the Typology of Manifest Destiny*. St. Louis, Mo.: Washington University Gallery of Art, 1992.

Tall Tales of Davy Crockett: The Second Nashville Series of Crockett Almanacs, 1839–1841. Introduction by Michael A. Lofaro. Knoxville: University of Tennessee Press, 1987.

Tanselle, G. Thomas. *Guide to the Study of United States Imprints*. Cambridge, Mass.: Belknap Press of Harvard University Press, 1971.

Tate, Michael L. *The Frontier Army in the Settlement of the West*. Norman: University of Oklahoma Press, 1999.

Tompkins, Jane. *West of Everything: The Inner Life of Westerns*. New York: Oxford University Press, 1992.

———. *Sensational Designs: The Cultural Work of American Fiction, 1790–1860*. New York: Oxford University Press, 1985.

Turner, Frederick Jackson. *Rereading Frederick Jackson Turner: "The Significance of the Frontier in American History," and Other Essays*. With commentary by John Mack Faragher. New York: H. Holt and Co., 1994; New Haven, Conn.: Yale University Press, 1998.

Wagner, Henry R., Charles L. Camp, and Robert H. Becker, eds. *The Plains and the Rockies: A Critical Bibliography of Exploration, Adventure, and Travel in the American West, 1800–1865*. San Francisco: John Howell Books, 1982.

Wallmann, Jeffrey M. *The Western: Parables of the American Dream*. Lubbock: Texas Tech University Press, 1999.

Watts, Edward, and David Rachels. *The First West: Writing from the American Frontier, 1776–1860*. New York: Oxford University Press, 2002.

White, Richard. *The Frontier in American Culture: An Exhibition at the Newberry Library, August 26, 1994–January 7, 1995*. Berkeley: University of California Press, 1994.

Wilson, R. L. *Buffalo Bill's Wild West: An American Legend*. New York: Random House, 1998.

Winship, Michael. *American Literary Publishing in the Mid-Nineteenth Century: The Business of Ticknor and Fields*. Cambridge: Cambridge University Press, 1995.

Wrobel, David M. *Promised Lands: Promotion, Memory, and the Creation of the American West*. Lawrence: University Press of Kansas, 2002.

Zboray, Ronald J. *A Fictive People: Antebellum Economic Development and the American Reading Public*. Oxford: Oxford University Press, 1992.

INDEX

A Note on the Types

The text of Books on the Frontier *is composed in Miller, a Scotch-style face designed by Matthew Carter in 1997 for Carter & Cone Type, Inc., and inspired by Edinburgh typefounder William Miller's Pica Roman No. 2, first used in 1809 for an edition of John Dryden edited by Sir Walter Scott. The captions are set in Interstate, designed by Tobias Frere-Jones in 1993 for the Font Bureau, Inc., and based on the signage alphabets of the United States Federal Highway Administration. The display type is Jason Wood, digitized by Dan X. Solo from an old Victorian wood type for Dover Publications, Inc., in 2000.*

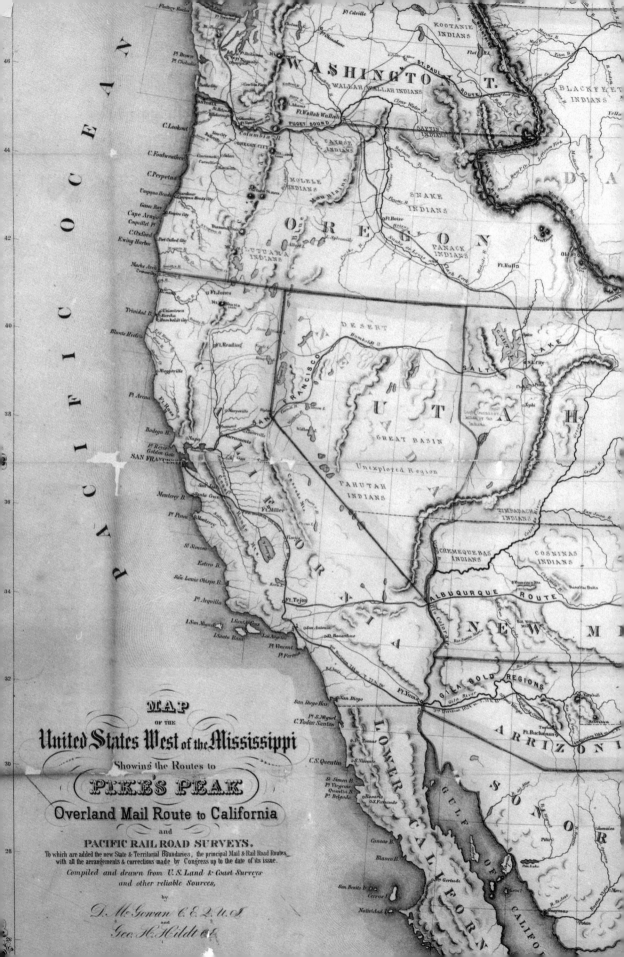

MAP
OF THE
United States West of the Mississippi
Showing the Routes to
PIKE'S PEAK
Overland Mail Route to California
and
PACIFIC RAIL ROAD SURVEYS,
To which are added the new State & Territorial Boundaries, the principal Mail & Rail Road Routes
with all the arrangements & corrections made by Congress up to the date of its issue.

Compiled and drawn from U.S. Land & Coast Surveys
and other reliable Sources,

by

D. McGowan C.E. 2. U.S.
and
Geo. H. Hildt C.